For Phil,
who always believes in me

MARKING TIME

MARKING TIME

Christian Rituals for All Our Days

Linda Witte Henke

MOREHOUSE PUBLISHING

Morehouse Publishing
P.O. Box 1321
Harrisburg, PA 17105

Morehouse Publishing is a division of The Morehouse Group.

Cover Design by Laurie Westhafer

Library of Congress Cataloging-in-Publication data

Henke, Linda Witte.
   Marking time : Christian rituals for all our days / Linda Witte Henke
     p. cm.
   ISBN 0-8192-1859-6 (alk. paper)
    1. Occasional services. I. Title.
BV199.O3 H38 2001
265—dc21   00-067874

Printed in the United States of America

01 02 03 04 05 06 07 08 09   10 9 8 7 6 5 4 3 2 1

Contents

II. CONSECRATION

III. ENCOURAGEMENT

IV. COMFORT

Preface

Each time my husband or I leave home, whether en route to the neighborhood grocery store or to a business meeting halfway around the world, we kiss and speak the words of our hearts: "I love you!" Each night as we retire to our bedroom, my husband and I make a game of calling our two dogs up onto the bed for a time of play and cuddling before sleep. In their simplest forms, these are rituals that shape our experiences of life.

Within hours of the deadly explosion, people of all ages and beliefs rushed to the site of what once was the Alfred P. Murrah Federal Building, there to leave memorial tokens of a sorrow too deep to name. The horrors of Columbine were not even fully known when youth and parents began to assemble in a nearby park to light candles, cling to one another, and assemble tokens of their shock and grief. In life and in death, in times of joy and in times of sorrow, we are creatures of ritual who long for ways to mark the significance of the life events and experiences that shape who we are and who we will yet become.

The presentation of an award marks the achievement of excellence. The shifting of a tassel signals the completion of one adventure and the beginning of another. The exchange of rings gives tangible expression to promises of lifelong commitment. Although life's events and experiences can certainly happen without the benefit of ritual, ritual invites us into fuller appreciation of the significance of those events and experiences.

I confess that my interest in ritual began early in life. My mother tells of arriving home from the hospital to the crowd of neighborhood children I had assembled on the front porch to welcome my baby sister. Even at the tender age of seven, I guess, I instinctively recognized that an addition to a family changes things.

My early instincts have been affirmed through participation in rituals ranging from baptisms to campfire sing-alongs, from confirmations to sorority inductions, from award banquets to ordinations.

Somewhere along the way, first as a lay religious leader working with youth and more recently as a parish pastor ministering to people in the various times and seasons of life, I began to recognize that we experience many more significant events in our lives than our culture has rituals to recognize. And so, as the years have passed, I have increasingly found myself crafting rituals to mark occasions of significance in the lives of friends, family, and parishioners.

More recently, participants in those rituals have begun to inquire about the availability of rituals for other life events and experiences. A participant in a ritual marking a friend's miscarriage asked about a ritual to celebrate the homecoming of an adopted child. Someone who accompanied a friend to a ritual blessing of pets asked about a ritual for when a pet dies. The sadness of children participating in a ritual marking the dissolution of their parents' marriage suggested the need for a ritual to affirm the insolubility of the covenant binding parent and child. A participant in a ritual for blessing a friend's home wistfully remarked that she wished she had had a ritual for when they had moved her mother-in-law out of her home and into an assisted-care residence. Someone who participated in a bedside ritual for their dying loved one later asked about a ritual to mark the anniversary of their loved one's death.

Marking Time is a collection of rituals to mark the significance of daily life experiences, from conception and birth to illness and death. Although there are many forms of ritual expression, the form of my expression is unabashedly Christian. I draw heavily on scripture because I believe these sacred writings have the power to speak with new relevance to each generation. I draw on the church's liturgical patterns because I believe daily life rituals need to be an adjunct to the worship life of the faith community, not a substitute for it. I encourage the incorporation of tangible symbols because I believe our experiences of the spiritual are made memorable in the material. I prompt the use of touch, through the sharing of the peace and the laying on of hands, because I believe these acts are reminiscent of the divine touch that shaped and formed us and called us to life.

Introduction

Because I've found that although many people hunger for ritual, they are not conversant in the practice of it, each of the offerings in *Marking Time* is introduced with recommendations to aid in that rite's use—selecting an occasion and/or site, recruiting leaders, preparing participants, and so forth. Each rite is camera-ready, that is, ready to be photocopied and used by the participants.

Some additional considerations, common to most ritual observances, may also be helpful:

❧ Participation ought always to be invited, never coerced. Accept that not everyone will feel comfortable participating. Respect their discomfort and choices.

❧ Interruption is the enemy of meaningful ritual. Take appropriate steps to protect this bit of sacred experience from the interruptions of radio and television, telephones and doorbells, pagers and cellular phones, and so forth.

❧ Recognize that most people are overstimulated by the demands and pace of life today. Dim lights to signal movement into a different way of being. Make use of visual aids (such as a cross, a candle, an open Bible, and so forth) to create a sense of sacred space. Allow for times of silence so that participants may quiet their thoughts and center their hearts for experiences of the Holy.

❧ Preparation is a way to demonstrate respect for the God we will encounter in ritual. Before scheduling a ritual's use, take time to read through the rite and assemble whatever items might enhance participants' experiences. Be mindful in your selection of a site and in your preparation of the site for ritual use. If the rite will be observed in conjunction with another event or gathering, ensure that someone is attending to those details. Consider making one photocopy of the rite so that you can personalize it by writing in names and circling appropriate word choices in the text of the rite. Then, make copies of the rite for each participant.

❧ Be sensitive in your recruitment of leaders and readers, mindful that the ability to preside with compassion and grace is not limited to the oldest or most accomplished. Take time to go over the rite with those who are the focal point of the ritual action so they will know what is involved and feel at ease in their participation. So that they may have opportunity to prepare for their respective roles, make copies of the rite available in advance to the leader, reader(s), and those who are the focal point of the ritual.

❧ Be thoughtful in your decision of whom to include in each ritual observance. In most cases, you'll want to be guided by the preferences of those who are the focal point for the rite. Recognize that many of these rites mark the significance of tender and intimate life experiences and are not intended to be public events; in fact, widening the circle beyond close friends and family will rob the rite of its deepest meaning.

❧ Music is a powerful addition to ritual observance. Although the inclusion of musical selections is beyond the scope of this resource, be alert to opportunities for incorporating appropriate musical selections into your use of these rites.

❧ And, finally, remember that God comes to us in the unexpected. Be diligent in preparing for a ritual's use but flexible in your experience of it. Open your heart to surprise and make room for spontaneity.

I

CELEBRATION

In My Mother's Womb
Celebrating Pregnancy

Whether planned or unplanned, pregnancy marks the beginning of a remarkable partnership with God in the creation of life. This rite invites reflection on the significance of that partnership and solicits mindful commitment to it. Intended for use within a small circle of close family and friends, the rite is well-suited for use in conjunction with a celebratory meal, perhaps at the time the pregnancy is announced.

Encourage the expectant parents to prepare for the rite by selecting a symbol to mark the significance of the pregnancy (perhaps a family Bible in which their baby's birth will be recorded or a baby book in which they will record their child's growth and development). Recruit a trusted friend or family member to lead the rite (ideally, someone other than a grandparent, since grandparents will want to participate fully in the rite). So that they may familiarize themselves with their respective roles, make copies of the rite available in advance to the leader and the expectant parents.

When it is time to begin, invite participants to gather in a circle around the expectant parents. Make copies of the rite available for all participants.

Leader: The Lord be with you!
All: And also with you!

Leader: O Lord, you have searched me and known me.
All: You know when I sit down and when I rise up; you discern my thoughts from far away.

Leader: You search out my path and my lying down, and are acquainted with all my ways.
All: Even before a word is on my tongue, O Lord, you know it completely.

Leader:	You hem me in, behind and before, and lay your hand on me.
All:	Such knowledge is too wonderful for me; it is so high that I cannot attain it.
Leader:	For it was you who formed my inward parts; you knit me together in my mother's womb.
All:	I praise you, for I am fearfully and wonderfully made. Wonderful are your works; that I know very well. *(Psalm 139:1–6, 13–14)*
Leader:	*(addressing the community)* We gather on this day to celebrate God's creative work in generating new life in _____.
	(addressing expectant parents) What symbol do you offer as a sign of your gratitude to God for this gift of new life?

The parent(s) may offer a symbol and describe briefly its significance.

Leader:	*(addressing expectant mother)* _____ , will you prepare for this new life by exercising care for your body as the vessel for its growth and development?
Mother:	I will, and I ask God to help me.
Leader:	*(addressing expectant father)* _____ , will you prepare for this new life by demonstrating care for your partner's physical and emotional well-being?
Father:	I will, and I ask God to help me.
Leader:	*(addressing expectant parents)* _____ , will you prepare for this new life by tending to your relationship with each other, that your child may be welcomed into a home that is furnished with consideration and respect, affection and joy?
Parents:	We will, and we ask God to help us.

Leader: Let us pray.

                God of all that was, is, and ever shall be, make your
                presence known to _____ as they
                prepare for this new life you are creating. Give them
                patience in their waiting, joy in their anticipation,
                and mutual affection for each other as they ready
                their lives and hearts to welcome this gift of life. Pro-
                tect the fetus and parents throughout the days of this
                pregnancy, that childbirth may be cause for celebra-
                tion and joy. In the name of your son, Jesus, through
                whom your love is being birthed in each of us.

All: Amen! May it be so!

*Participants may encircle the expectant parents and place hands on their
heads and shoulders.*

Leader: I am confident of this, that the one who began a good
                work among you will bring it to completion in the
                day of Jesus Christ! *(Philippians 1:6)*

Participants withdraw their hands.

Leader: The peace of the Lord be with you always!
All: And also with you!

        The rite concludes with a sharing of the peace.

The Lord Is Good
Celebrating the Birth of a Child

Although the birth of a child is ordinarily a cause for celebration, it can also be a time of intense physical exhaustion and emotional vulnerability for the child's parents. Exercise sensitivity in discerning whether the parents would welcome the opportunity to participate in a rite celebrating their child's birth.

This rite is intended for use soon after a child's birth. It may be used within a small, intimate circle of close family and friends, but, with the consent of the parents, that circle might be enlarged to also include attending medical personnel. Recruit one friend or family member (perhaps a grandparent) to lead the rite and another to read the lesson from scripture. Make copies of the rite available for all participants.

As soon as the rite has concluded, encourage participants to honor the parents and child by making a timely departure.

Leader:	The Lord be with you!
All:	And also with you!
Leader:	Make a joyful noise to the Lord, all the earth!
All:	Worship the Lord with gladness; come into his presence with singing!
Leader:	Know that the Lord is God. It is he that made us, and we are his.
All:	We are his people, and the sheep of his pasture.
Leader:	Enter his gates with thanksgiving, and his courts with praise. Give thanks to him and bless his name.
All:	For the Lord is good; his steadfast love endures forever, and his faithfulness to all generations. *(Psalm 100)*
Reader:	A reading from the holy gospel according to Luke, the eighteenth chapter: "People were bringing even in-

fants to him that he might touch them; and when the disciples saw it, they sternly ordered them not to do it. But Jesus called for them and said, 'Let the little children come to me, and do not stop them; for it is to such as these that the kingdom of God belongs.'" *(Luke 18:15–16)*

The gospel of the Lord!
All: Thanks be to God!

Leader: Let us pray.

Creating God, we are privileged to celebrate your gift of new life in this child. Fill our hearts with the spirit of your love, so that we may receive him/her with the kind of hospitality that Jesus demonstrated in gathering children into his arms. God, in your mercy,

All: Hear our prayer!

Leader: Sustaining God, we give you thanks for the parents of this child. Bless their devotion to one another so that they may fully share in the joys and sorrows they will experience in parenting this child. Sensitize us to the challenges they will face so that we may be sources of encouragement and support for them. God, in your mercy,
All: Hear our prayer!

Leader: Redeeming God, look with compassion on the whole human family. Break down the walls that separate us and unite us in bonds of love, so that we may work together to accomplish your purposes. We pray in the name of your Son, Jesus Christ our Lord.
(Inspired by *Lutheran Book of Worship*, 44.)
All: Amen! May it be so!

Participants may place their hands on the couple and their child.

Leader: May God bless you and keep you!
                  May God's face shine on you and be gracious to you!
                  May God look on you with favor and give you peace!

Hands are withdrawn.

Leader: The peace of the Lord be with you always!
All: And also with you!

The rite concludes with a sharing of the peace.

That We May See Your Joy
Marking an Infant's Homecoming

In these days of greatly abbreviated hospital stays, an infant's home-coming may well be the first opportunity for family and friends to celebrate the child's birth. This rite invites participants into greater mindfulness of God's goodness in creating this child and of the community's responsibility in receiving this child into its midst.

Although designed for use at the time the infant first arrives home with his/her parents, the rite could also be used in conjunction with a staged reenactment of that event. The rite is most appropriately observed in the home of the infant's parents, provided that someone other than the parents is willing and able to assume the responsibility of host(ess). Since the homecoming event is an especially intimate one, only very close family and friends should be invited to participate, and even then, only those specifically identified by the parents for inclusion.

Go over the rite in advance with the parents and alert them to the opportunity to introduce their child and share whatever information about him/her that they consider appropriate. Also discuss with them the gift of welcome called for in the rite and ensure that a gift will be available. While the gift should have symbolic significance, it need not be expensive or extravagant. (For example, the offering of an heirloom quilt or handmade afghan or receiving blanket would be especially appropriate, as would a family Bible that includes space for the recording of births and other life events.)

Recruit one friend or family member to lead the rite and another to read the scripture lesson, and another (perhaps the child's grand-parent or older sibling) to present the gift, and if desired, offer a brief statement of joy and welcome. So that they may prepare for their respective roles, make copies of the rite available in advance to the parents, the leader, the reader, and the presenter.

Although an infant's homecoming is a time of celebration, it may not be the most opportune time for a party. Consider serving meager refreshments at the rite so that guests will not be tempted to linger and overtax parents and/or child. So as not to add to the stresses already being experienced by parents and child (both birth and adoptive), communicate clearly to participants the nature and scope of the gathering.

When it is time to begin the rite, invite those gathered to stand and form a circle around the parents and their child. Make copies of the rite available to all participants.

Leader:	The Lord be with you!
All:	And also with you!

Leader:	Rejoice with Jerusalem, and be glad for her; all you who love her, rejoice with her in joy.
All:	Let the Lord be glorified, so that we may see your joy!

Leader:	May you nurse and be satisfied from her consoling breast; may you drink deeply with delight from her glorious bosom.
All:	Let the Lord be glorified, so that we may see your joy!

Leader:	For thus says the Lord: I will extend prosperity to her like a river; you shall nurse and be carried on her arm, and dandled on her knees.
All:	Let the Lord be glorified, so that we may see your joy!

Leader:	Thus says the Lord:
Women:	As a mother comforts her child, so I will comfort you! *(Isaiah 66:10–13)*
Men:	As a father welcomes his child, so I will welcome you!
All:	Let the Lord be glorified, so that we may see your joy!

Reader:	A reading from Psalm 22:
	Yet, it was you who took me from the womb;
	you kept me safe on my mother's breast.
	On you I was cast from my birth,
	and since my mother bore me, you have been my God.
	I will sing of your steadfast love,
	O Lord I will proclaim your faithfulness to all generations. *(Psalm 22:9–10, 89:1)*
	The word of the Lord!

All:	Thanks be to God!

Leader: *(addressing the community)* We are gathered to cele-
            brate a homecoming, the welcoming of a child into
            the hearts and lives of his/her parents and into the
            arms of this community of family and friends.

            (addressing the parents) Who is the child we will wel-
            come?

*Time is allowed for the parents to introduce the child, sharing informa-
tion they feel is appropriate (date of birth and/or adoption, place of
birth, what his/her name will be, and so forth.). When the introduction
is concluded, the rite is continued.*

Leader: What shall be the symbol of this homecoming?

            *Time is allowed for presentation of a gift of welcome by
            a representative of the group. After the presentation is
            made, the rite is continued.*

Leader: Let us pray. Gracious God,
All: may we guide this child with wisdom and insight,
            that he/she may explore with confidence and learn
            with joy.
Mother: When we are unsure,
Father: when our own confidence fails,
All: parent us, O God, with reminders of your abiding
            love and presence.

Leader: Open our hearts,
Mother: sustain our commitment,
Father: empower our faithfulness,
All: that we may be ever mindful of our calling to serve
            you by caring well for this child.

Leader: In the name of Jesus, who embraced children in
            welcome and blessing,
All: Amen! Thanks be to God!

Leader: May God bless us and keep us,
All: That we may make this child welcome among us!

| Leader: | May God's face shine on us and be gracious to us, |
| All: | That we may illumine the path of this child's journey to life in you! |

| Leader: | May God look on us with favor and give us peace, |
| All: | That we may see your joy unfolding in this child! |

| Leader: | The peace of the Lord be with you always! |
| All: | And also with you! |

The rite concludes with a sharing of the peace.

Gift of Belonging
The Naming of A Child

Much thought typically goes into the selection of the name by which a child is called. This rite acknowledges the significance of the process by which a child receives this primary gift from his/her parents. It also invites awareness that the one being named is a unique individual.

The rite is intended for use among a circle of the parents' family and friends. It may be used in conjunction with a celebratory meal, perhaps as part of the first gathering of family and friends after the child's birth or adoption.

Recruit one friend or family member to lead the rite and another one (or two) to read the scripture lessons. Alert the child's parents that they will be asked to name the child and will be given an opportunity, if they desire, to describe the significance of the name they have chosen. So that the leader, reader(s), and parents may have the opportunity to prepare for their respective roles, make copies of the rite available to them in advance.

When it is time for the rite to begin, invite those gathered to stand and form a circle around the parents and child. Make copies of the rite available to all participants.

Leader: The Lord be with you!
All: And also with you!

Leader: *(addressing the community)* Naming is a sign of our belonging to one another. To be named is to be known, to be claimed by another. Naming this child signals our commitment to a future yet to be defined.

Reader #1: A reading from Exodus, the third chapter:

            But Moses said to God, "If I come to the Israelites and say to them, 'The God of your ancestors has sent me to you,' and they ask me, 'What is his name?' what shall I say to them?" God said to Moses, "I AM who I am . . . This is my name forever, and this my title for all generations." *(Exodus 3:13–14a, 15b)*

The word of the Lord!

All: Thanks be to God!

Leader: "I am who I am"—or, in a literal translation of the original Hebrew, "I will be who I will be." In the name, we are introduced to the essence of God,
Mother: Known and unknown,
Father: Revelation and mystery,
All: Changing and evolving—endless possibility.

Leader: *(addressing the community)* We are gathered here to give name to the new life God has entrusted to

_____ .

(addressing the parents) By what name will this child be called into relationship?
Parent(s): His/her name shall be _____ .

(If desired, the parents may briefly describe the significance of the name they have selected for their child.)

Leader: In this name, we are introduced to the essence of this child,
Mother: Known and unknown,
Father: Revelation and mystery,
All: Changing and evolving—endless possibility.
Mother: *(addressing the child)* We welcome the child that you are!
Father: We rejoice in the man/woman you will become!
All: We celebrate the gift of our belonging to one another!

Leader: *(addressing the community)* This gathering of family and friends is indeed a blessing, but God would have us understand that this child's belonging extends beyond this circle.

Reader #2:	A reading from Isaiah, the forty-third chapter:

Thus says the Lord, he who created you, O Jacob, he who formed you, O Israel: Do not fear, for I have redeemed you; I have called you by name, you are mine. When you pass through the waters, I will be with you; and through the rivers, they shall not overwhelm you; when you walk through fire you shall not be burned, and the flame shall not consume you. For I am the Lord your God. . . . You are precious in my sight, . . . and I love you. *(Isaiah 43:1–4)*

The word of the Lord!

All:	Thanks be to God!

Leader:	_____'s name and person are known to God!
Mother:	May God direct his/her growing and becoming.
Father:	May God protect his/her coming and going.
All:	"I will be who I will be," says the Lord our God.
Mother:	Known and unknown!
Father:	Revelation and mystery!
All:	Changing and evolving—endless possibility!

Leader:	Cherished by God who created him/her, loved by parents who have embraced him/her, shaped by the community that surrounds him/her:
Mother:	*(addressing the child)* May God bless you and keep you!
Father:	May God's face shine on you and be gracious to you!
All:	May God look on you with favor and give you peace!

Leader:	In the name of the Triune God, who binds us together in one circle of belonging:
All:	Amen! Thanks be to God!

Leader:	The peace of the Lord be with you always!
All:	And also with you!

The rite concludes with a sharing of the peace.

Living Water
Preparation for Baptism

Participation in the sacrament of Holy Baptism marks the commitment of one's life to God. As such, it is an event that holds significance for the duration of one's life.

Recognizing that baptism into Christ marks one's entrance into Christian community, this rite is designed to aid family and friends in their preparation for a loved one's baptism. Drawing on the multifaceted meanings evoked by images of water, the rite invites participants into mindful reflection on the lasting significance of baptism in the lives of all baptized children of God.

The rite may appropriately be used a day or two prior to the baptism within the context of a family meal or larger gathering of family and friends. Recruit one friend or family member to lead the rite and another to read the scripture lesson. So that they may have opportunity to prepare for their roles, make copies of the rite available in advance to the leader and reader.

Prepare for the rite by draping a small table with a white cloth. Place on the table a candle, a bowl and pitcher of water, and a cross and/or an open Bible. When it's time to begin, light the candle, ensure the person to be baptized is in close proximity to the table, and invite participants to assemble in a circle around the person and the table. Make copies of the rite available to all participants.

Leader: The Lord be with you!
All: And also with you!

Leader: Have mercy on me, O God,
All: According to your steadfast love and abundant mercy.

Leader: Create in me a clean heart, O God,
All: And put a new and right spirit within me.

Leader: Restore to me the joy of your salvation,
All: And sustain in me a willing spirit.

Leader:	O Lord, open my lips,
All:	And my mouth will declare your praise.
	(Psalm 51:1, 10, 12)

During a reading of the lesson, a representative slowly pours the water from the pitcher into the bowl.

Reader: A reading from the gospel according to John, the fourth chapter:

A Samaritan woman came to draw water, and Jesus said to her, "Give me a drink." . . . The Samaritan woman said to him, "How is it that you, a Jew, ask a drink of me, a woman of Samaria?". . . Jesus answered her, "If you knew the gift of God, and who it is that is saying to you, 'Give me a drink,' you would have asked him, and he would have given you living water." The woman said to him, "Sir, you have no bucket, and the well is deep. Where do you get that living water?". . . Jesus said to her, "Everyone who drinks of this water will be thirsty again, but those who drink of the water that I will give them will never be thirsty. The water that I will give will become in them a spring of water gushing up to eternal life." The woman said to him, "Sir, give me this water, so that I may never be thirsty." *(John 4:7–15)*

The gospel of the Lord!

All: Thanks be to God!

Leader: *(addressing the community)* In this gathering in anticipation of _____ 's rebirth through the waters of holy baptism, we are called to mindfulness of the role of water in our lives. Water is the means by which we are delivered from the womb into life. It is used to wash and make clean. Water is a source of refreshment and revitalization. It is both a gentle stream and raging flood, capable of both nurturing life and destroying it. In the waters of baptism, we are joined in the death of Christ, in order that we might also be joined in the new life of Christ's resurrection.

Let us pray.

	Gracious God, we pray that you would wash _____ in the flood of your grace,
All:	That his/her baptism may be a spring of living water gushing up to eternal life.
Leader:	Creating God, we pray that you would create a new heart in _____,
All:	That his/her baptism may be a spring of living water gushing up to eternal life.
Leader:	Redeeming God, we pray that you would put a new and a right spirit in _____,
All:	That his/her baptism may be a spring of living water gushing up to eternal life.
Leader:	Sustaining God, we pray that you would nurture _____ in the faith,
All:	That his/her baptism may be a spring of living water gushing up to eternal life.
Leader:	Triune God—Father, Son, and Holy Spirit—bind us to _____ through faith in you and restore in us true joy in your salvation,
All:	That our baptisms may be springs of living water gushing up to eternal life.
Leader:	In the name of Christ, we pray,
All:	Amen! Thanks be to God!
Leader:	The Lord be with you!
All:	And also with you!

The rite concludes with a sharing of the peace.

This Good Work in You
Affirmation of Baptism

Whenever young children are brought forward for baptism, parents and baptismal sponsors are enjoined to bring those children up in the faith and to help them remember their baptisms. When adults come forward for baptism, we offer them a similar directive. Unfortunately, we provide no resources to encourage their faithfulness in doing so.

There are, of course, numerous occasions in the life of the church when opportunities may be provided for corporate and/or public affirmation of baptism. This rite, however, is intended for use within a small circle of family or close friends who serve as one's family-of-choice. The rite takes advantage of this intimate setting to encourage affirmations of the individual's unfolding baptismal identity.

Although the rite may be used at any time, it is especially appropriate for use annually, on the date of one's baptismal anniversary. Since baptism is God's lifelong gift to us, this rite may appropriately be used with young children, youth, and both young and mature adults. If desired, it may be preceded by a celebratory meal.

To prepare for the rite, drape a small table with a white cloth and assemble an arrangement of available baptism mementos (baptismal candle and/or certificate, banner, dress, photographs, and so forth). As needed, supplement the arrangement with a candle, a cross or open Bible, and a small bowl or shell of water.

Recruit one friend or family member to lead the rite and another one (or two) to read the scripture lessons. Alert the Affirmand that he/she will be asked to dip his/her fingers in the water and trace the sign of the cross on his/her forehead. So that the leader, reader(s), and Affirmand have opportunity to prepare for their respective roles, make copies of the rite available to them in advance.

When it is time to begin, light the candle and ensure that the Affirmand is in close proximity to the table of baptism mementos. Then, invite participants to stand and form a circle around the Affirmand. Make copies of the rite available to all participants.

Leader:	The Lord be with you!
All:	And also with you!
Reader #1:	A reading from St. Paul's letter to the Romans, the sixth chapter:
	Do you not know that all of us who have been baptized into Christ Jesus were baptized into his death? Therefore we have been buried with him by baptism into death, so that, just as Christ was raised from the dead by the glory of the Father, so we too might walk in newness of life. *(Romans 6:3–4)*
	The word of the Lord!
All:	Thanks be to God!
Leader:	*(addressing the community)* In Holy Baptism, our gracious Heavenly Father liberates us from sin and death by joining us to the death and resurrection of our Lord Jesus Christ. We are born children of a fallen humanity; in the waters of baptism, we are re-born children of God and inheritors of eternal life. By water and the Holy Spirit, we are made members of the church, which is the body of Christ. As we live in Christ and among God's people, we grow in faith, love, and obedience to the will of God.
	(addressing Affirmand) Do you desire to celebrate God's faithful presence in your life by affirming the promises made on the day of your baptism?
Affirmand:	I do, and I ask God to help me.
Leader:	I ask you, along with this community of believers, to profess faith in the Triune God, in whose name you were baptized.
All:	I believe in God, the Father almighty, creator of heaven and earth.

I believe in Jesus Christ, his only Son, our Lord.
He was conceived by the power of the Holy Spirit
and born of the virgin Mary.
He suffered under Pontius Pilate,
was crucified, died, and was buried.
He descended into hell.
On the third day he rose again.
He ascended into heaven
and is seated at the right hand of the Father.
He will come again to judge the living and the dead.
I believe in the Holy Spirit,
the holy Catholic Church,
the communion of saints,
the forgiveness of sins,
the resurrection of the body,
and the life everlasting. Amen.

Reader #2:   A reading from St. Paul's letter to the Philippians, the first chapter:

I thank my God every time I remember you, constantly praying with joy in every one of my prayers for all of you, because of your sharing in the gospel from the first day until now. I am confident of this, that the one who began a good work among you will bring it to completion by the day of Jesus Christ. *(Philippians 1:3–6)*

The word of the Lord!

All: Thanks be to God!

Leader: *(addressing the Affirmand and indicating the water in the bowl or shell)* In remembrance of the good work begun in you in baptism, I invite you to dip your fingers into this water and trace on your forehead the sign of the cross.

The Affirmand traces the sign of the cross on his/her forehead.

All:	*(addressing the Affirmand)* Child of God, you have been sealed by the Holy Spirit and marked with the cross of Christ forever!
Leader:	*(addressing the community)* How do we see _____ 's baptismal promises coming to fulfillment in his/her life?

Time is allowed for a brief sharing of ways Affirmand's baptismal identity is unfolding. When the sharing has concluded, the rite continues.

The leader places his/her hand on the Affirmand's head; others may place their hands on the Affirmand's head or shoulders.

Leader:	Let us pray. We praise you, O God, for freeing your sons and daughters from the power of sin and raising us up to new life in you. Increase in _____ the gift of your Holy Spirit: the spirit of wisdom and understanding, the spirit of counsel and might, the spirit of knowledge and the fear of the Lord, the spirit of joy in your presence. We pray in the name of your Son Jesus Christ, through whose death and resurrection your work is coming to completion in us.
All:	Amen! May it be so!

Hands are withdrawn.

Leader:	*(addressing the Affirmand)* May God bless you and keep you,
All:	That all may see your good works and glorify your Father in heaven!
Leader:	May God's face shine on you and be gracious to you,
All:	That your light may shine before others!
Leader:	May God look on you with favor and give you peace,
All:	That the good work, begun in you in baptism, may come to faithful completion!

Leader: The peace of the Lord be with you always!
All: And also with you!

The rite concludes with a sharing of the peace.

(This rite incorporates elements from the service of Holy Baptism found in *Lutheran Book of Worship*, 121–125.)

The Household of God
Affirming the Covenant between Parent and Child

Most parents and their children are aware of the commitment that binds them together. On occasion, however, that presumed awareness is best articulated with clarity and intentionality.

Emphasizing mutual accountability in the parent-child relationship, this rite may be used annually (perhaps in conjunction with a celebration of Mother's Day, Father's Day, or a special family holiday) or situationally (perhaps when the parents have decided to separate or divorce or when the family is faced with some other significant challenge or transition). To prepare for the rite, assemble a few mementos of the family's life together and arrange them with a candle and open Bible in a prominent place in the location in which the rite will be observed.

Recruit one friend or family member (someone other than the parents and children participating in the rite) to lead the rite and another to read the scripture lesson. So that they may have opportunity to prepare for their respective roles, make copies of the rite available in advance to the leader, reader, parents, and children.

When it is time for the rite to begin, light the candle and invite participants to stand, encouraging children to stand with their parents.

Leader:	The Lord be with you!
All:	And also with you!

Leader:	Give ear, O my people, to my teaching; incline your ears to the words of my mouth.
All:	Tell the coming generation of the glorious deeds of the Lord and the wonders that he has done.

Leader:	Teach my commands to your children, so that the next generation may know them and tell them to their children,
All:	So that they may not forget the works of God but keep his commandments and set their hope in God. *(based on Psalm 78:1, 4–7)*

Reader:	A reading from St. Paul's letter to the Ephesians, the fourth and fifth chapters:

So then, putting away falsehood, let all of us speak the truth to our neighbors, for we are members of one another. Be angry but do not sin; do not let the sun go down on your anger, and do not make room for the devil. Let no evil talk come out of your mouths, but only what is useful for building up, as there is need. Put away from you all bitterness and wrath and anger and wrangling and slander, together with all malice, and be kind to one another, tenderhearted, forgiving one another, as God in Christ has forgiven you. Therefore be imitators of God, as beloved children, and live in love, as Christ loved us and gave himself up for us, a fragrant offering and sacrifice to God. *(Ephesians 4:25–27, 29, 31–5:2)*

The word of the Lord!

All:	Thanks be to God!

Leader:	*(addressing the community)* Scripture clearly views children as a gift, as a blessing entrusted to the mindful stewarding of parents. Parents are enjoined to love their children and to provide for their well-being. By instruction and example, parents are to teach their children the ways of God. Parents are not to provoke their children to anger, but to strive to administer loving discipline that will encourage their children's growth toward maturity.

In situations where parents are not married or where dissolution of marriage provides the occasion for this rite, the leader may include the following statement.

While the commitment of the parents to each other in marriage normally provides the context within which mothers and fathers embrace the parental covenant, no circumstance should be permitted to compromise the bond mothers and fathers share with their children. Commitment to the well-being of their children demands that parents demonstrate a spirit of cooperation and mutual respect toward each another.

We have come together to affirm the covenant relationship between _____
and his/her/their child(ren), _____ .

(addressing the parent[s]) _____ ,
are you prepared to affirm your commitment to covenant relationship with your child(ren)?

Parent(s):   I am/we are, and I/we ask God to help and guide me/us.

Leader: Do you promise to honor and respect each other and to fully cooperate with each other in the parenting of your child(ren)?

Parents: We do, and we ask God to help and guide us.

Leader: Do you promise to love your child(ren) and provide for his/her/their physical, emotional, intellectual, and spiritual well-being, both in the provision of resources and opportunities and in the appropriate restriction of them?

Parent(s):   I/we do, and I/we ask God to help and guide me/us.

Leader: Do you promise, both by instruction and example, to teach your child(ren) the ways of God and encourage his/her/their growth in Christian faith and discipleship?

Parent(s):   I/we do, and I/we ask God to help and guide me/us.

Leader: Do you promise to administer loving, appropriate discipline purposed in your child(ren)'s growth toward maturity?

Parent(s):   I/we do, and I/we ask God to help and guide me/us.

Leader: *(addressing the community)* Scripture also clearly views children as having responsibilities to their parents. Children are to love their parents and treat them with honor and respect. Children are to be obedient to their parents, submitting themselves to the guidance and direction their parents provide. Children are charged to follow the commands of God so that they are prepared to one day teach those commands to their own children.

(addressing child[ren]) _____ , are you prepared to affirm your commitment to the covenant relationship with your parent(s)?

Child(ren):   I am/we are, and I/we ask God to help and guide me/us.

Leader: Do you promise to love your parent(s) and treat him/her/them with honor and respect?

Child(ren):   I/we do, and I/we ask God to help and guide me/us.

Leader: Do you promise to obey your parent(s), submitting yourself to his/her/their guidance and direction?

Child(ren):   I/we do, and I/we ask God to help and guide me/us.

Leader: Do you promise to grow in Christian faith and discipleship, following the commands of God?

Child(ren):   I/we do, and I/we ask God to help and guide me/us.

Leader: *(addressing both parent[s] and child[ren])* Do you promise to live as members of one another and of Christ and, in word and deed, to build up one another in love?

Parent(s) and
Children: We do and we ask God to help and guide us.

Parent(s) and child(ren) are invited to join hands.

Leader: Let us pray.

O God, you made us in your own image and redeemed us through Jesus your Son. Look with compassion on the whole human family; break down the

walls that separate us and unite us in bonds of love that, together, we may work to accomplish your purposes on earth. In your mercy, we pray,
(Adapted from *Lutheran Book of Worship*, 44.)

All: Shape us into one household of God!

Leader: O God, who imaged our relationship with you as that of child and parent, bind children and parents together in loving relationships with one another. Enable children to honor their parents and treat them with love and respect. Give parents wisdom, insight, and compassion, that they may parent well the children you have entrusted to their care. Bless children and parents with affection for one another and devotion to you. In your mercy, we pray,

All: Shape us into one household of God!

Leader: O God, who like a mother gathers us to yourself and like a father welcomes us into your wide embrace, gather _____ and his/her/their child(ren), _____ , into covenant relationship with one another. Bless their commitment to one another and to you, that they may share with each other the joys of Christian fellowship for as long as they live. In your mercy, we pray,

All: Shape them into one household of God!

Leader: In the name of Christ, we pray. Amen.

Parent(s) and child(ren) may let go of hands.

Leader: May God bless us and keep us!
Parent(s) and
Child(ren): May God's face shine on us and be gracious to us!
All: May God look on us with favor and give us peace!

Leader: The peace of the Lord be with you always!
All: And also with you!

The rite concludes with a sharing of the peace.

God of Endless Possibility
Celebrating Personal Achievement

Some achievements, such as graduations, are greeted with much pomp and circumstance. Other equally significant achievements generate little, if any, notice. This rite provides a means for celebrating all manner of personal achievements—from learning to ride a bike to being selected for the team or school play, from earning a scholarship to completing a book manuscript, from performing an unsolicited deed of kindness to completing a landscaping project—all within the context of God's gifts coming to amazing fulfillment in us.

The rite is designed for use within an intimate gathering of close family and friends, perhaps in conjunction with a celebratory meal or a savoring of the honored person's favorite snack or dessert. If possible, display some symbol of the achievement and/or hold the rite in a place of relevance to the achievement.

Recruit one friend or family member to lead the rite and another to read the scripture lessons. Alert the person whose achievement is being celebrated that he/she will have opportunity during the rite to announce the achievement and describe its significance. So that they may have opportunity to prepare for their respective roles, make copies of the rite available in advance to the leader, reader, and person(s) whose achievement(s) is/are being recognized.

When it is time to begin, invite all participants to assemble (standing or sitting, depending on what seems most appropriate to the setting). Make copies of the rite available to all participants.

Leader: The Lord be with you!
All: And also with you!

Leader: Make a joyful noise to the Lord, all the earth!
All: Worship the Lord with gladness; come into his presence with singing!

Leader: Know that the Lord is God. It is he that made us, and we are his.
All: We are his people, and the sheep of his pasture.

Leader: Enter his gates with thanksgiving, and his courts with praise. Give thanks to him, bless his name.

All: For the Lord is good; his steadfast love endures forever, and his faithfulness to all generations. (*Psalm 100*)

Reader: A reading from St. Paul's first letter to the Corinthians, the twelfth chapter:

Now there are varieties of gifts, but the same Spirit; and there are varieties of services, but the same Lord; and there are varieties of activities, but it is the same God who activates all of them in everyone. To each is given the manifestation of the Spirit for the common good. (*I Corinthians 12:4–8*)

And a reading from St. Paul's letter to the Ephesians, the fourth chapter:

I therefore . . . beg you to lead a life worthy of the calling to which you have been called, with all humility and gentleness, with patience, bearing with one another in love, making every effort to maintain the unity of the Spirit in the bond of peace. There is one body and one Spirit, just as you were called to the one hope of your calling, one Lord, one faith, one baptism, one God and Father of all, who is above all and through all and in all. But each of us was given grace according to the measure of Christ's gift. (*Ephesians 4:1b–7*)

The word of the Lord!

All: Thanks be to God!

Leader: (*addressing the community*) God fashions us in love, equips us with gifts, and empowers us to achieve great things. What achievement will we celebrate on this day?

Time is allowed for the sharing of milestones and achievements and a brief description of their significance. When the sharing is concluded, the rite continues.

Leader: Let us pray.

God of endless possibility, we praise you for fashioning us in your image and equipping us with gifts that demonstrate your love for us. We celebrate your power at work in _____ and pray that you give him/her/them gratitude for your goodness and joy in his/her/their achievement. God, in your mercy,

All: Give us grace according to the measure of Christ's gift.

Leader: God of endless possibility, we praise you for the wondrous diversity of gifts and abilities you make available to our community through one another. Open our hearts to these varied expressions of your goodness and empower us to celebrate that goodness in ourselves and others. God, in your mercy,

All: Give us grace according to the measure of Christ's gift.

Leader: God of endless possibility, we praise you that, through the gift of your Son, each day is an unfolding of new opportunities for us to love and serve you. Give us the wisdom to discern your will and the courage to embrace it, that the gifts and abilities you entrust to us may be used for the good of all. God, in your mercy,

All: Give us grace according to the measure of Christ's gift.

Leader: In the name of Christ, we pray,
All: Amen. May it be so!

| Leader: | May the God of endless possibility gather us in love, equip us with grace, and empower us to service, |
| All: | According to the measure of Christ's gift! |

| Leader: | The peace of the Lord be with you always! |
| All: | And also with you! |

The rite concludes with a sharing of the peace.

That Your Joy May Be Complete
Marking an Engagement for Marriage

The decision of two people to marry takes place within a wider context that includes the family and friends of both parties. Grounding the couple's decision in God's command for us to love one another, this rite solicits the support of family and friends for the couple in their commitment to each other.

The rite is intended for use within a small circle of close family and friends, ideally with representatives of both families present. It could appropriately be used in conjunction with a celebratory meal or reception at which the couple's engagement is formally announced.

The rite calls for the couple to offer a symbol of their intention to marry. Although the man's traditional presentation of an engagement ring to his beloved would certainly be appropriate, other possibilities would be equally so. Possibilities include a Bible (with space to record significant events in the couple's future life together), a special cross, a candle, a plaque, or a memento from the extended family of each party.

Recruit one friend or family member to lead the rite and another to read the scripture lesson. Ensure the availability of family representatives and review with them their role. So that they may have opportunity to prepare for their respective roles, make copies of the rite available in advance to the leader, reader, family representatives, and the couple.

When it is time to begin, invite participants to stand and form a circle around the couple. Make copies of the rite available to all participants.

Leader: The Lord be with you!
All: And also with you!

Leader: Make a joyful noise to the Lord, all the earth!
All: Worship the Lord with gladness; come into his presence with singing!

Leader:	Know that the Lord is God. It is he that made us, and we are his.
All:	We are his people, and the sheep of his pasture.
Leader:	Enter his gates with thanksgiving, and his courts with praise. Give thanks to him and bless his name.
All:	For the Lord is good; his steadfast love endures forever, and his faithfulness to all generations. *(Psalm 100)*
Reader:	A reading from the gospel according to John, the fifteenth chapter:

And Jesus said, "As the Father has loved me, so I have loved you; abide in my love. If you keep my commandments, you will abide in my love, just as I have kept my Father's commandments and abide in his love. I have said these things to you so that my joy may be in you, and that your joy may be complete. This is my commandment, that you love one another as I have loved you." *(John 15:9–12)*

The gospel of the Lord!

All:	Thanks be to God!
Leader:	*(addressing the community)* Just as many factors affect the decision of two people to become engaged, so also do many factors affect the couple's ability to embrace the lifelong commitment of marriage. We are gathered on this occasion to celebrate the joy of _____ and _____ in pledging themselves to each other for marriage and to offer our support for their commitment to each other.

(addressing the couple) _____ and _____, what intentions will you declare on this day?

Man: *(addressing the woman's parent[s] or other representa-*
tive of her family of origin) I declare to you my love for
_____ and my intention to live in
faithfulness to her for the rest of my life. So that our
joy in each other may be complete, will you give your
blessing to this intention and to our love for one another?

Woman's
Parent(s): *(addressing man)* _____ , I/we celebrate your love for _____ and give
my/our blessing to your intention. May you know
complete joy in one another!

Woman: *(addressing the man's parent[s] or other representative*
of his family of origin) I declare to you my love for
_____ and my intention to live in
faithfulness to him for the rest of my life. So that our
joy in each other may be complete, will you give your
blessing to this intention and to our love for one another?

Man's
Parent(s): *(addressing woman)* _____ , I/we
celebrate your love for _____ and
give my/our blessing to your intention. May you
know complete joy in one another!

Man and
Woman: *(addressing other family and friends)* We declare to
you our love for each other and our intention to live
in faithfulness to each other for the rest of our lives.
So that our joy in each other may be complete, will
you give your blessing to this intention and to our
love for one another?

Family and
Friends: *(addressing man and woman)* _____
and _____ , we celebrate your love
and give our blessing to your intention. May you
know complete joy in one another!

The man and woman face each other and join hands.

Man:	*(addressing woman)* _____, before God and with the blessing of our family and friends, I declare my love for you and promise to be faithful to you for the rest of my life.
Woman:	*(addressing man)* _____, before God and with the blessing of our family and friends, I declare my love for you and promise to be faithful to you for the rest of my life.
Leader:	*(addressing man and woman)* What do you offer as a symbol of your intention?

Time is allowed for the man and woman to offer a symbol of their intention to marry. If desired, they may share the significance of the symbol they offer. When the sharing is concluded, the rite continues.

Leader:	Let us pray.
	God of love, who wills that no one should be alone, we praise you for the gift of your goodness unfolding in _____ and _____ 's relationship. Empower them in their loving, sustain them in their intentions, and nurture them in their commitment to one another and to you. May they abide in your love,
All:	And may your joy be complete in them!
Leader:	God of love, who fashioned humankind in your own image and declared us good, we praise you for the gift of your goodness made known in relationships of commitment among your sons and daughters. Bless our unions, give us generous and forgiving hearts, and increase our delight in one another and in you. May we abide in your love,
All:	And may your joy be complete in us!
Leader:	God of love, who places us in families and communities, we remember before you those who are experiencing isolation or loneliness. Make us mindful of one another, sensitive to the inclusion of others, and

	willing to be used as instruments of your love for all
	people. May we abide in your love,
All:	And may your joy be complete in us!

Leader:	We pray in the name of Christ our Lord, whose sacri-
	fice on the cross makes it possible for us to abide in
	your love.
All:	Amen! Thanks be to God!

The couple joins hands. Parents or other family representatives place their hands on the couple's joined hands. Others join hands to form a circle around the couple.

Leader:	May God bless you and keep you!
	May God's face shine on you and be gracious to you!
	May God look on you with favor and give you peace!
All:	Amen!

Hands are withdrawn.

| Leader: | The peace of the Lord be with you always! |
| All: | And also with you! |

The rite concludes with a sharing of the peace.

By Wisdom a House Is Built
Blessing of a Dwelling

Among the many places where we spend our time, few have the capacity to shape our lives in quite the way that our dwellings do. This rite provides an opportunity to invoke God's blessing on this place of formation, that God's love may be a welcomed presence, that God's ways may be a conscious intention, and that God's blessing may be received with mindful gratitude.

Although this rite could certainly be used within the family circle, it is designed for use within a wider circle of friends and extended family, perhaps within the context of a housewarming. Recruit one friend or family member to lead the rite and another to read the brief scripture lesson. Also recruit five friends or family members to assemble and present the symbolic gifts of blessing (a loaf of bread, a container of salt, a bottle of wine, a candle, and a quilt, blanket, or afghan). So that they may prepare for their respective roles, make copies of the rite available in advance to the leader, reader, and presenters.

When it is time to begin, invite participants to assemble in a central area of the dwelling. Make copies of the rite available to all participants.

Leader:	The Lord be with you!
All:	And also with you!
Leader:	Unless the Lord builds the house,
All:	Those who build it labor in vain. *(Psalm 127:1)*
Leader:	By wisdom a house is built, and by understanding it is established;
All:	By knowledge its rooms are filled with all precious and pleasant riches. *(Proverbs 24:3)*
Leader:	*(addressing the community)* We come together on this occasion to seek God's blessing on the dwelling of _____. Let us pray.

Fill this space, O God, with a spirit of gratitude. Furnish it with the comfort of your presence and adorn it with expressions of your compassion for all people. Make this dwelling a safe haven for the one(s) who live(s) here and a place of renewal and refreshment for those who come to visit, that it may ever be a temple where your will is honored and your name is praised. In the name of Christ, we pray,

All: Amen! May it be so!

Leader: *(addressing the one[s] whose dwelling is being blessed)*
                    What hopes and dreams do you have for this dwelling?

Time is allowed for an informal sharing. When the sharing has concluded, the rite continues.

Leader: *(addressing person[s] whose dwelling is being blessed)*
                    _____, we are privileged to share your hopes and dreams for this dwelling. These gifts are signs of our hope for God's blessing of your life in this place.

A loaf of bread is presented.

Friend #1:   This gift of bread is a sign of our hope that you will have blessings sufficient to sustain your life and generosity sufficient to share those blessings with others.

A portion of salt is presented.

Friend #2:   This gift of salt is a sign of our hope that this dwelling may be seasoned with sufficient love and respect, that it may spill over and add flavor to the world around you.

A bottle of wine is presented.

Friend #3:   This gift of wine is a sign of our hope that this dwelling may be a place where, in the midst of life's sorrows, you may find plentiful cause for joy and celebration.

A lighted candle is presented.

Friend #4:   This candle is a sign of our hope that this dwelling may be a place where hope burns bright, chasing away the darkness of evil and pointing the way to Jesus, our one true light.

A quilt/blanket/afghan is presented.

Friend #5:   This quilt/blanket/afghan is a sign of our hope that you will be surrounded in this dwelling by God's love and empowered to share that love with others.

Leader: *(addressing person[s] whose dwelling is being blessed)* Will you receive these gifts and commit yourself to living out their intentions?

Dweller(s):   I/we do, and I/we ask God to help and guide me/us.

Leader: Let us pray.

O God, you made us in your own image and redeemed us through Jesus your Son. Look with compassion on the whole human family. Break down the walls that separate us and unite us in the bonds of your love that, together, we may work to accomplish your purposes. In the name of Christ, we pray, (Adapted from *Lutheran Book of Worship*, 44.)

All: Amen! May it be so!

Leader: By wisdom a house is built, and by understanding it is established;

All: By knowledge its rooms are filled with all precious and pleasant riches. *(Proverbs 24:3)*

Leader: May the Spirit of Almighty God, Father, Son, and Holy Spirit, rest upon this place and on those who dwell here.

All: Amen! Thanks be to God!

| Leader: | The peace of the Lord be with you always! |
| All: | And also with you! |

The rite concludes with a sharing of the peace.

To Love and To Honor
Affirmation of Marriage

Although much fanfare is frequently associated with the joining of a couple in marriage, precious little effort is invested in helping husbands and wives live out the promises they make to each other on the day of their wedding. This rite is purposed in giving couples an opportunity to affirm their commitment to each other and to their marriage.

Although couples may appropriately affirm their commitment at any time and in many ways and places, this particular rite is especially well suited for use in conjunction with a celebration of the couple's wedding anniversary or for the consecration of a civil marriage ceremony. Recruit one friend or family member (someone who models commitment to marriage) to lead the rite and another one or two friends or family members to read the scripture lessons. So that they may have opportunity to prepare for their respective roles, make copies of the rite available in advance to the leader, the reader(s), and the couple.

To prepare for the rite, cover a small table with a white cloth and arrange on it mementos of the couple's life together (marriage certificate or announcement, wedding gown, service bulletin, unity candle, wedding and other photos, and so forth). If necessary, supplement the arrangement to include a tall white candle and a cross or open Bible.

When it's time to begin, light the candle and ask the couple to stand in close proximity to the table. Invite other participants to stand and form a circle around the couple. Make copies of the rite available to all participants.

Please note that, with minor modification, this rite can be adapted for use within the context of a worship service, perhaps for an occasion when couples are annually given the opportunity to affirm their marriage commitment. Such a service might appropriately begin with a time for confession and absolution, move toward proclamation of God's word in a brief sermon, and culminate in a celebration of the Holy Communion.

| Leader: | The Lord be with you! |
| All: | And also with you! |

Leader: Let us pray.

Gracious God, you fashioned us in your own image and redeemed us through Jesus, your Son. Look now, we pray, on the whole human family. Break down the walls that separate us and unite us in the bonds of love, that all people may live in harmony with one another and in service to you, through Jesus Christ our Lord. Amen.
(Adapted from *Lutheran Book of Worship*, 44.)

Reader #1:   A reading from St. Paul's first letter to the Corinthians, the thirteenth chapter:

If I speak in the tongues of mortals and of angels, but do not have love, I am a noisy gong or a clanging cymbal. And if I have prophetic powers, and understand all mysteries and all knowledge, and if I have all faith, so as to remove mountains, but do not have love, I am nothing. If I give away all my possessions, and if I hand over my body so that I may boast, but do not have love, I gain nothing.

Love is patient; love is kind; love is not envious or boastful or arrogant or rude. It does not insist on its own way; it is not irritable or resentful; it does not rejoice in wrongdoing, but rejoices in the truth. It bears all things, believes all things, hopes all things, endures all things. Love never ends.

For now we see in a mirror, dimly, but then we will see face to face. Now I know only in part; then I will know fully, even as I have been fully known. And now faith, hope, and love abide, these three; and the greatest of these is love. *(I Corinthians 13:1–8a, 12–13)*

The word of the Lord!

All: Thanks be to God!

Reader #2:	A reading from the holy gospel according to John, the fifteenth chapter:

Jesus said, "I am the vine, you are the branches. Those who abide in me and I in them bear much fruit, because apart from me you can do nothing. If you abide in me, and my words abide in you, . . . you bear much fruit and become my disciples. As the Father has loved me, so I have loved you; abide in my love. If you keep my commandments, you will abide in my love, just as I have kept my Father's commandments and abide in his love. I have said these things to you so that my joy may be in you, and that your joy may be complete." *(John 15:5, 7a, 8–11)*

The gospel of the Lord! |
| All: | Thanks be to God! |
| Leader: | *(addressing the community)* Affirmation of the marriage covenant does not suggest that a man and woman discard the past and start over. Rather, participation in this rite of affirmation indicates that, in spite of what has gone before and what yet may come, this man and this woman commit their lives anew to one another and to the covenant called into being on the day of their wedding.

(addressing the couple) Do you desire to affirm your commitment to each other? |
Couple:	We do, and we ask God to help and guide us.
Leader:	*(addressing husband)* _____, will you continue in your commitment to _____? Will you continue to love her, comfort her, honor and keep her, in sickness and in health, in poverty and in wealth?
Husband:	I will, and I ask God to help me.

| Leader: | *(addressing wife)* _____, will you continue in your commitment to _____? Will you continue to love him, comfort him, honor and keep him, in sickness and in health, in poverty and in wealth? |
| Wife: | I will, and I ask God to help me. |

Leader:	*(addressing couple)* You may join hands and face each other as you repeat after me.
Husband:	*(addressing wife)* I renew my promise to be your loving partner and to be faithful to you until death parts us.
Wife:	*(addressing husband)* I renew my promise to be your loving partner and to be faithful to you until death parts us.
All:	*(addressing couple)* May God sustain you in your commitment to one another, that you may find new delight in each other and grow in your devotion to each other until your life's end!

| Leader: | *(addressing the community)* Let us thank God for the love that creates and sustains us each day. |

A brief silence is observed for reflection.

| Leader: | Loving God, we praise you for creating us as members of one human family. Teach us to appreciate the diversity in which you have created us, that we may love all people and honor all expressions of human relationship. God, in your mercy, |
| All: | Hear our prayer! |

| Leader: | Gracious God, we praise you for your ability to call your new creation to life, even in the broken places of our lives. When our hearts ache with the pain of failures in self or others, assure us of your eagerness to forgive and remind us that your will is for all people to live together in love and in honor. God, in your mercy, |
| All: | Hear our prayer! |

| Leader: | Embracing God, make your presence known to those who are alone through no desire of their own. Use us to communicate your compassion, so that all might feel loved and honored. God, in your mercy, |
| All: | Hear our prayer! |

| Leader: | Faithful God, we praise you for the covenant that binds us securely to you. Bless the bond that unites _____ and _____, that they may serve one another in love and in honor for as long as they live. God, in your mercy, |
| All: | Hear our prayer! |

| Leader: | We entrust all for whom we pray to your loving embrace, through your Son, Jesus Christ our Lord. |
| All: | Amen! Thanks be to God! |

The leader may place his/her hand on the couple's joined hands.

| Leader: | May God bless you and keep you, |
| All: | That you may be united in your commitment to one another! |

| Leader: | May God's face shine on you and be gracious to you, |
| All: | That you may find delight in your affection for one another! |

| Leader: | May God look on you with favor and give you peace, |
| All: | That you may serve one another, in love and in honor, all the days of your life! |

The leader's hand is withdrawn.

| Couple: | *(addressing the community)* The peace of the Lord be with you always! |
| All: | And also with you! |

The rite concludes with a sharing of the peace.

From Generation to Generation
Marking the Gathering for Family Reunion

Family reunions can be occasions for great joy. They can also be occasions for expressing grief and for attending to unresolved family issues. This rite creates a place to acknowledge God's faithfulness among the generations as they, together, experience the joys and sorrows of their familial connection.

The rite is appropriately enacted at the reunion site, perhaps soon after family members have assembled. Recruit one family member to lead the rite and enable his/her preparation by providing him/her with an advanced copy of the rite. Alert other family members to the opportunity within the rite to name recently departed family members and those who have recently been incorporated into the family.

When it is time to begin, invite participants to stand and assemble in a central location. Make copies of the rite available to all participants.

Leader: The Lord be with you!
All: And also with you!

Leader: God is our refuge and strength.
All: From generation to generation, we will recount your praise!

Leader: Upon you I have leaned from my birth; it was you who took me from my mother's womb.
All: From generation to generation, we will recount your praise!

Leader: Oh God, from my youth you have taught me; and I still proclaim your wondrous deeds.
All: From generation to generation, we will recount your praise!

Leader: Do not cast me off in the time of my old age; do not forsake me when my strength is spent.
All: From generation to generation, we will recount your praise!

Leader: From generation to generation, our God is a God of salvation.

All: Then, our mouth was filled with laughter, and our tongue with shouts of joy.
(Psalm 46:1; 71:6, 9, 17; 79:13; 126:2)

Leader: *(addressing the community)* God places us in families in order that we might experience the blessings of mutual respect, nurture, affection, and joy.

With each gathering, we become freshly aware of family members who are no longer with us. What family members have completed their earthly journey since our last reunion?

Time is allowed for a naming of the departed, either informally as loved ones come to mind or more formally as a roll call by date of death. When naming has concluded, the rite continues.

Leader: God is our refuge and strength! *(Psalm 46:1)*

All: From generation to generation, we will recount your praise! *(Psalm 79:13)*

Time is allowed for a brief silence to remember departed family members.

Leader: With each gathering, we are reminded that God's goodness continues to be revealed. What family members has God added to our number since the last reunion?

Time is allowed for a naming of new births or adoptions (perhaps with such identifying information as "daughter of _____ and granddaughter of _____"). If desired, this may also include a naming of those who have entered the family by marriage (perhaps with such identifying information as " _____, spouse of _____ " or " _____, stepson of _____"). When the naming concludes, the rite continues.

Leader:	God is our refuge and strength! (*Psalm 46:1*)
All:	From generation to generation, we will recount your praise! (*Psalm 79:13*)
Leader:	Let us pray.
	Heavenly Father,
	Look with compassion, we pray, on the whole human family. Take away the arrogance and hatred that infect our hearts. Break down the walls that separate us. Unite us in bonds of love, that, through our unity in you, all generations may live together peaceably and serve you faithfully. From generation to generation, O God, (Adapted from *Lutheran Book of Worship*, 44.)
All:	We place our trust in you!
Leader:	Look with compassion, we pray, on those who grieve. Console them with a clear sense of your presence in their sorrow. Move their hearts to thankfulness for joys known in loved ones who have gone to be with you. Assure them with knowledge of your great love for all people, that they may be at peace in entrusting their loved ones to your eternal care. From generation to generation, O God,
All:	We place our trust in you!
Leader:	Look with compassion, we pray, on all generations of those who love and serve you. May children know they are loved and cherished. May youth be blessed with adults to guide, encourage, and show faith in them. May young adults experience both confidence in self and trust in you. May adults know the privilege of productive work, joyful leisure, and relationships of mutual affection and trust. May the elderly be treated with respect and honor. From generation to generation, O God,
All:	We place our trust in you!

Leader:	Look with compassion, we pray, on the _____ family. Let children and parents have mutual respect for one another. Let a spirit of kindliness prevail among brothers and sisters. Living in the love and forgiveness you shower on all your people, may this family experience genuine affection for one another. Hear us, O God, for we place our trust in you!
All:	In the name of Christ, we pray, Amen! May it be so!
Leader:	From generation to generation,
All:	May God bless us and keep us!
Leader:	From generation to generation,
All:	May God's face shine on us and be gracious to us!
Leader:	From generation to generation,
All:	May God look on us with favor and give us peace!
Leader:	The peace of the Lord be with you always!
All:	And also with you!

The rite concludes with a sharing of the peace.

II

CONSECRATION

Praying Hands
Family Prayer

We hear much lament about the decline of family values, the erosion of close relationships between parents and children, and the reluctance of young people to embrace the Christian faith. Perhaps we have forgotten that values must be demonstrated in order to be passed on, that relationships must be cultivated in order to grow strong, and that young people must experience the faith in order to make it their own.

This simple ritual is based on the tradition of using the digits of one's hand to prompt mindful prayer. In this tradition:

❦ the thumb prompts us to pray for ourselves.

❦ the index finger prompts us to pray for those who point, direct, guide, and lead (such as parents, teachers, pastors, youth workers, and so forth).

❦ the middle finger prompts us to pray for those in positions of strength and authority (such as governing officials, employers, the police and/or military forces, the wealthy, and so forth).

❦ the ring finger prompts us to pray for those dear to our hearts (family, friends, neighbors, and so forth).

❦ the little finger prompts us to pray for those who are small or vulnerable (children, the ill or dying, the grieving, the poor, the oppressed, the environment, and so forth).

This practice—simple enough to be introduced with young children and profound enough to challenge even the most mature—encourages a mutual sharing of joys, sorrows, and concerns that is the essence of Christian community in all times and in every season of family life.

Although the rite is presented here in written form, daily repetition will quickly commit it to memory. When children are very young, an adult will need to take responsibility for leading the rite, but children should be invited to share the leadership role as soon as they are able. The rite is intended as a time of mutuality among family members of all ages. In appropriately articulating their joys, sorrows (including confession of wrongdoing), and concerns, adults demonstrate spiritual integrity and graciously invite children to prayerfully name their own life and faith experiences.

Leader: In the name of the Father, and of the Son, and of the Holy Spirit.

All: I love the Lord, because he has heard my voice and my supplications. Because he has inclined his ear to me, I will call on him as long as I live. *(Psalm 116:2)*

If desired, a devotional reflection may be read.

Leader: What joys shall we celebrate on this day?

Each participant, in turn, briefly expresses gratitude for the particular joys of his/her life.

All: We praise you, O God, for the joys of this day!

Leader: What sorrows shall we acknowledge on this day?

Each participant, in turn, briefly confesses the particular sorrows (including wrongdoings) of his/her day.

All: Comfort us, O God, with assurance of your compassion and forgiveness!

Leader: What concerns shall we lift up on this day?

    While holding with one hand each successive digit on the opposite hand, participants go around the circle, naming their concerns for self and others:

    ❧ *the thumb (prayers for one's self)*
    ❧ *the index finger (prayers for those who point, direct, guide, and lead)*

    ♭ *the middle finger (prayers for those in positions of strength and authority)*
    ♭ *the ring finger (prayers for those near and dear to us)*
    ♭ *the little finger (prayers for those who are small or vulnerable)*

All: Comfort us with your presence, O God, and send your healing love to those for whom we pray.

Leader: Lord, remember us in your kingdom and teach us to pray:
All: *(Traditional version)*

Our Father, who art in heaven,
hallowed be thy name, thy kingdom come,
thy will be done, on earth as it is in heaven.
Give us this day our daily bread;
and forgive us our trespasses
as we forgive those who trespass against us.
And lead us not into temptation,
but deliver us from evil.
For thine is the kingdom, and the power,
and the glory, forever and ever. Amen.

(Contemporary version)

Our Father in heaven,
hallowed be your name,
your kingdom come,
your will be done,
on earth as in heaven
Give us today our daily bread.
Forgive our sins
as we forgive those
who sin against us.
Save us from the time of trial
and deliver us from evil.
For the kingdom, the power,
and the glory are yours,
now and forever. Amen.

Participants may join hands.

Leader: May God bless us and keep us. May God's face shine on us and be gracious to us. May God look on us with favor and give us peace.

All: Amen! Thanks be to God!

Leader: The peace of the Lord be with you always!

All: And also with you!

The rite concludes with a sharing of the peace.

This I Know
Preparation for a Child's First Day of School

When a child starts school, he/she is often taking an initial step in the long journey toward independence. A child's first day of school is, therefore, a significant event in the lives of both parent and child.

For even the most adventuresome child and the most courageous parent, a child's first day of school can produce feelings of heightened anxiety. Acknowledging the reality of unknown factors, this rite offers opportunities for child and parents to be assured by affirmation of God's companionship on the child's journey. Building on a phrase from a well-known children's song, the rite incorporates a blessing of the child and of some of the school items that will accompany the child on his/her adventure.

Before using the rite, take a few minutes to discuss it with the child. Talk about the song from which the rite draws its theme and emphasize how he/she can carry that song's message with him/her as a reminder of God's love in every time and place. Explain that the rite is a way for those who love him/her to convey to him/her God's blessing as he/she begins school.

The rite may be used in conjunction with a family meal or an informal gathering of close friends or family. Recruit a friend or family member to lead the rite. Prepare for the rite by assembling items that will accompany the child to school (such as clothing, book bag, paper and pencils, and so forth).

When it is time to begin, invite participants to stand and form a circle around the young student. Make copies of the rite available for all participants.

Leader:	The Lord be with you!
All:	And also with you!

Leader:	In this is love, not that we loved God but that he loved us and sent his Son to be the atoning sacrifice for our sins!
All:	Jesus loves me, this I know!

Leader:	See what love the Father has given us, that we should be called children of God!
All:	Jesus loves me, this I know!
Leader:	All who obey God's commandments abide in him, and he abides in them!
All:	Jesus loves me, this I know!
Leader:	God is love, and those who abide in love abide in God, and God abides in them!
All:	Jesus loves me, this I know! *(I John 2:2; 3:1, 24; 4:16b)*
Leader:	*(addressing the community)* _____ is about to begin a new adventure—his/her first day of school—and we are gathered to mark the significance of that day.

School is a time to make new friends and to experience new things. What do we know about _____'s first day of school?

Time is allowed for the parents to assure the child with what is known about his/her first day of school, reiterating information that has already been shared with the child on previous occasions. (Where is the school located [have they visited?]? Who will take him/her? Who will his/her teacher be [have they met?]? Who will his/her classmates be [has he/she met any of them?]? What will he/she wear [is there a new or special outfit or article of clothing?]? What supplies will he/she take with him/her? How long will he/she be gone? Who will come to take him/her home?) As parents discuss tangible items (such as clothing or supplies), they may place those items in the center of the circle.

Leader:	*(addressing the child)* _____, shall we ask God to bless these special things that will accompany you on your first day of school?

The community places its hands on the assembled items.

Leader: Gracious God, we ask that you would bless these items that will accompany _____ on his/her first day of school. Bless these books/notebooks/pencils so that he/she will know that you are with him/her as he/she learns wonderful things about your creation. Bless this book bag, so that he/she will know that you will be with him/her in his/her new experiences. Bless these articles of clothing, so that he/she will know that you are surrounding him/her with your love. Use these things to give _____ confidence for what he/she will learn and assurance in what he/she already knows: that he/she is loved by you and supported by his/her family and friends. In the name of Jesus, we pray,

All: Amen.

Hands are withdrawn from the items. The leader's hand is placed (lightly) on the child's head or shoulder.

Leader: _____, may God bless you and keep you,

All: For Jesus loves you, this we know!

Leader: May God's face shine on you and be gracious to you,

All: For Jesus loves you, this we know!

Leader: May God look on you with favor and give you peace;

All: For Jesus love you this we know!

The leader's hand is withdrawn.

Leader: The peace of the Lord be with you always!

All: And also with you!

The rite concludes with a sharing of the peace.

I Am the Vine
Marking the Beginning of a School Year

For some students, the beginning of a school year marks a return to dearly loved friends and activities. For others, the beginning of a school year marks a return to a place that holds painful memories of loneliness, isolation, disappointment, or failure. For all students, the beginning of a school year marks an opportunity to encounter new people and attitudes, to acquire knowledge and make choices, to claim growth through encounter with experiences of success and failure.

Although adults typically have high hopes and expectations for the young people in their lives, they may not seek out opportunities to articulate those hopes and expectations. Although parents love their children and devote themselves to looking after their best interests, they may not communicate that love and concern in direct and memorable ways. Using an event of significance in the life of young people, this rite creates an opportunity for those conversations to begin. It also provides an opportunity to convey God's blessing to those we love.

Although their behaviors may give off signals to the contrary, most young people instinctively recognize the importance of beginning the school year well. Discuss this rite with your child or youth to discern his/her willingness to participate. Suggest that he/she invite a few of his/her peers (and their families) to also participate in the rite.

The rite may be appropriately used in conjunction with a celebratory meal—in this case, perhaps an end-of-summer cookout or picnic. When using the rite for one child, invite one friend or family member to serve as leader and another one (or two) to read the scripture lessons. When using the rite for several children or youth, invite someone known to all (perhaps a school counselor or church youth group advisor) to lead the rite and ask a couple of the parents to read the lessons. So that the leader and reader(s) may have opportunity to prepare for their roles, make a copy of the rite available to them in advance.

As the rite begins, make copies of the rite available to all participants.

Leader: The Lord be with you!
All: And also with you!

Reader #1:   A reading from I Corinthians, chapter 13:

If I speak in the tongues of mortals and of angels, but do not have love, I am a noisy gong or a clanging cymbal. And if I have prophetic powers, and understand all mysteries and all knowledge, and if I have all faith, so as to remove mountains, but do not have love, I am nothing. If I give away all my possessions, and if I hand over my body so that I may boast, but do not have love, I gain nothing.

Love is patient; love is kind; love is not envious or boastful or arrogant or rude. It does not insist on its own way; it is not irritable or resentful; it does not rejoice in wrongdoing, but rejoices in the truth. It bears all things, believes all things, hopes all things, endures all things. Love never ends.

For now we see in a mirror, dimly, but then we will see face to face. Now I know only in part; then I will know fully, even as I have been fully known. And now faith, hope and love abide, these three, and the greatest of these is love. *(I Corinthians 13:1–8a, 12–13)*

The word of the Lord!

All: Thanks be to God!

Leader: *(addressing student[s])* A new school year is a somewhat ambiguous undertaking. You will have opportunities to learn more about God's creation and reasons to recognize that you will never understand all things. You will have opportunities to experience pride in your achievements and frustration with your human limitations. You will be exposed to the expectations of others and to something of what it means to be true to yourself. Like life, this school year will almost certainly be a time of both opportunity and challenge, both confidence and uncertainty, both success and failure, both joy and sorrow. Who among us faces the opportunities and challenges that a new school year will bring?

Time is allowed for the student(s) to identify himself/herself/themselves by name and the nature of his/her/their educational endeavors (for example, "I'm Tom Smith, and I'll be in third grade at Washington Elementary" or "I'm Sue White, and I'm a graduate student at Tech State.") When the student(s) has/have been identified, the rite continues.

Reader #2: A reading from the gospel according to John, the fifteenth chapter:

Jesus said, "I am the vine, you are the branches. Those who abide in me and I in them bear much fruit, because apart from me you can do nothing. If you abide in me, and my words abide in you, . . . you bear much fruit and become my disciples. As the Father has loved me, so I have loved you; abide in my love. If you keep my commandments, you will abide in my love, just as I have kept my Father's commandments and abide in his love. I have said these things to you so that my joy may be in you, and that your joy may be complete." *(John 15:5, 7a, 8–11)*

The gospel of the Lord!

All: Thanks be to God!

Leader: *(addressing the group)* What hopes does this community have for its student(s)?

All: *(addressing the student[s])* Our hope is that you will learn:

  ❧ a deeper understanding of God's creation and a deeper appreciation for the goodness in which you were created.

  ❧ respect for self and compassion for others.

  ❧ openness to ideas and people unfamiliar to you.

🎵 a willingness to listen to others, but the courage to think for yourself.

🎵 the importance of faith in God and the value of service to others.

Time is allowed for participants to briefly articulate other hopes they have for the student(s). When the hopes have been shared, the rite continues.

Leader: Let us pray.

God of all wisdom, we praise you for wisely gifting us with sons and daughters. Give to each one a clear sense of your love, that they may feel your presence supporting them throughout this school year. Guide their choices, direct their quest for knowledge, bless their relationships, and use their successes and failures as opportunities to grow in understanding of who you would have them be. Continue, we pray, to shape them as branches of the one true vine, that they may ever walk in the way of Christ, grow strong in your Spirit's love for all people, and know the complete joy of life in you.

All: In the name of Christ, we pray, Amen.

Leader: *(addressing the student[s]):*
May God bless you and keep you.
May God's face shine on you and be gracious to you.
May God look on you with favor and give you peace.

All: Amen! Thanks be to God!

Leader: The Lord be with you!
All: And also with you!

The rite concludes with a sharing of the peace.

Wonderfully Made
When an Adolescent Begins to Date

Although our bodies and sexuality are ingredients to the goodness in which we were created, they constitute aspects of adolescent development that are sources of anxiety for both parents and youth. Intended for use when an adolescent begins to date, this rite celebrates the goodness of God's creation while encouraging the responsible stewardship of one's relationships and sexuality.

This rite is intended for use within a small circle of close family and friends, perhaps in conjunction with a celebratory meal. With minor modification, it can be adapted for use among a larger circle of multiple adolescents and their parents, perhaps in conjunction with a shared meal and/or guest speaker on a related theme. Recruit one friend or family member to lead the rite and another to read the lesson from scripture. So that they may have opportunity to prepare for their respective roles, make copies of the rite available in advance to the leader, reader, parents, and youth.

When it is time for the rite to begin, invite participants to stand and configure themselves so that each youth is with his/her parent(s). Make copies of the rite available to all participants.

Leader:	The Lord be with you!
All:	And also with you!
Reader:	O Lord, you have searched me and known me; it was you who formed me in my mother's womb.
All:	I will praise you, for I am fearfully and wonderfully made!
Leader:	You know when I sit down and when I rise up; you search out my path and are acquainted with all my ways.
All:	I will praise you, for I am fearfully and wonderfully made!
Leader:	You discern my thoughts from far away; even before a word is on my tongue, you know it completely.

All:	I will praise you, for I am fearfully and wonderfully made!
Leader:	Such knowledge is too wonderful for me; it is so high that I cannot attain it.
All:	I will praise you, for I am fearfully and wonderfully made!
Leader:	In every time and place, your hand shall lead me, your right hand hold me fast.
All:	I will praise you, for I am fearfully and wonderfully made!
Leader:	You will never let me go, for day and night, sunlight and darkness are all the same to you.
All:	I will praise you, for I am fearfully and wonderfully made!
Leader:	Wonderful are your works and ways; that I know very well.
All:	I will praise you, for I am fearfully and wonderfully made! *(Psalm 139:1–4, 6, 10, 12–14)*
Reader:	A reading from Genesis, the first chapter:

Then God said, "Let us make humankind in our image, according to our likeness; and let them have dominion over the fish of the sea, and over the birds of the air, and over the cattle, and over all the wild animals of earth, and over every creeping thing that creeps upon the earth."

So God created humankind in his image, in the image of God he created them; male and female he created them. God blessed them, and God said to them, "Be fruitful and multiply, and fill the earth and subdue it; and have dominion over [all creation]. And it was so. God saw everything that he had made, and indeed, it was very good. *(Genesis 1:26–28, 30b–31)*

The word of the Lord!

All:	Thanks be to God!

Leader: *(addressing the community)* Our human inclination in looking at ourselves is to criticize what we see. By contrast, the inclination of the One who fearfully and wonderfully made us is to look at us and declare, "You are very good."

At no point in our lives will that divine declaration ever change, for God loves us unconditionally and unerringly wants what is best for us. It is because God loves us and wants us to experience the joy of love that God plants within us a longing to be in close relationship with another, a longing that grows especially powerful during adolescence and young adulthood.

As the time has come when _____ will begin to date, we have gathered on this occasion to celebrate the goodness in which he/she/they was/were created, to affirm the goodness of his/her/their longing for love and relationship, and to ask God's guidance and direction for the choices and decisions he/she/they will face in the years ahead.

(addressing adolescent(s)) _____, do you recognize the goodness in which you were created and the goodness of the longing for relationship that God has entrusted to you?

Adolescent(s): Yes, for I know that I am fearfully and wonderfully made!

Leader: Do you recognize the goodness in which others were created and the goodness of the longing God has entrusted to them?

Adolescent(s): Yes, for I know that they, too, are fearfully and wonderfully made!

Leader:	Will you pledge yourself to the faithful stewarding of God's creation: To exercise care and respect for the physical, emotional, and spiritual well-being of yourself and others? To be mindful and responsible in the making of choices that will shape the futures of yourself and others? To honor the love in which you were created and by which God sustains your every breath?
Adolescent(s):	Yes, for I know that we are fearfully and wonderfully made!

Leader:	*(addressing parent[s])* _____, will you affirm your commitment to loving and responsible parenting during your child's adolescence? Will you set reasonable boundaries for this stage of your child's journey to adulthood, affording trust commensurate with his/her capacity for making responsible choices? Will you share with your child your values and convictions, while ensuring that he/she has the information necessary to make his/her own responsible choices? Will you model care and respect in your own relationships with self and others?
Parent(s):	Yes, for I/we know that I/we am/are fearfully and wonderfully made!

Leader:	*(addressing the community)* Will you demonstrate your love for _____ by committing yourself/yourselves to support him/her/them in the making of responsible choices that honor God's vision of goodness for all people?
All:	Yes, for we know that we are fearfully and wonderfully made!

Leader:	Let us pray.
	Creating God, we know that, in love, you fashioned us in your image and will for us to experience the goodness of loving relationships with you and others. Give parents wisdom, that they may offer helpful guidance and direction. Give youth insight, that they

may make choices that honor self and others and give glory to you. Give this community the willingness to provide encouragement and support. As _____ journey(s) toward adulthood, keep him/her/them ever mindful that he/she/they is/are as precious to you as your own beloved Son, in whose name we pray,

All: Amen.

Leader: May God bless us and keep us,
All: For we are fearfully and wonderfully made!

Leader: May God's face shine on us and be gracious to us,
All: For we are fearfully and wonderfully made!

Leader: May God look on us with favor and give us peace,
All: For we are fearfully and wonderfully made!

Leader: The peace of the Lord be with you always!
All: And also with you!

The rite concludes with a sharing of the peace.

A Light to My Path
Marking the Transition to Adult Driving Privileges

Few events have as profound an effect on family life as a teen family member's acquisition of a driver's license. This rite is designed to mark the significance of this occasion as a time of the teen's transition to greater freedom and responsibility and of the parents' diminished ability to protect and control their child.

Although this rite may be used as part of a celebration within the family unit, it is intended for use within a somewhat larger gathering that includes the youth's family and his/her close peers and their parents. In recognition that behaviors take shape within the context of community, this rite solicits commitments, not only from the youth acquiring the license, but also from that youth's parents and peers.

To lead the rite, recruit a trusted friend or family member (other than a parent) who embraces a commitment to responsible driving. Recruit another friend or family member to read the appointed scripture lesson. Go over the rite with the parents and enlist their willingness to have a set of car keys available for presentation to the youth. Go over the rite with the youth's peers and enlist their assistance in acquiring a special key chain for presentation during the rite. So that they may prepare for their respective roles, make copies of the rite available in advance to the leader, reader, parents, youth, and the youth's peers.

When it is time to begin, invite participants to stand. Make copies of the rite available to all participants.

Leader: The Lord be with you!
All: And also with you!

Leader: Teach me, O Lord, the way of your statutes, and I will observe it to the end. Turn my heart to your decrees, and not to selfish gain, give me life in your ways.
All: Your word is a lamp to my feet and a light to my path!

Leader:	Give me understanding that I may keep your laws and observe it with my whole heart.
All:	Your word is a lamp to my feet and a light to my path!
Leader:	My lips will pour forth praise, because you teach me your statutes. My tongue will sing of your promise, for all your commandments are right.
All:	Your word is a lamp to my feet and a light to my path! *(Psalm 119:33–34, 37, 105, 171–172)*
Reader:	A reading from St. Paul's first letter to the Corinthians, the thirteenth chapter:

If I speak in the tongues of mortals and angels, but do not have love, I am a noisy gong or a clanging cymbal. And if I have prophetic powers, and understand all mysteries and all knowledge, and if I have all faith, so as to remove mountains, but do not have love, I am nothing. If I give away all my possessions, and if I hand over my body so that I may boast, but do not have love, I gain nothing.

Love is patient; love is kind; love is not envious or boastful or arrogant or rude. It does not insist on its own way; it is not irritable or resentful; it does not rejoice in wrongdoing, but rejoices in the truth. It bears all things, believes all things, hopes all things, endures all things. Love never ends.

When I was a child, I spoke like a child; when I became an adult, I put an end to childish ways. For now we see in a mirror, dimly, but then we will see face to face. Now I know only in part; then I will know fully, even as I have been fully known. And now faith, hope, and love abide, these three; and the greatest of these is love. *(I Corinthians 13:1–8a, 11–13)*

The word of the Lord!

All:	Thanks be to God!
Leader:	*(addressing the community)* We are gathered to celebrate _____'s acquisition of an adult driver's license and to ask God's blessing on his/her use of this added privilege and responsibility. Are you committed to this intention?
All:	We are, and we ask God to help and guide us.
Leader:	*(addressing the youth)* _____, you have achieved the age of eligibility for independent operation of a motor vehicle. Are you prepared to commit yourself to responsible use of your license to drive?
Youth:	I am, and I ask God to help and guide me.
Leader:	Adult driving privileges come with numerous responsibilities. Do you pledge to obey all traffic laws and respond appropriately to all traffic signs, signals, and directives? Do you promise to be attentive, not only to your own driving but also to what is going on around you, so that you may contribute to the safety of all? Do you commit yourself to demonstrating consideration of others, even when they do not afford you that same consideration? And, since skill and judgment can only be acquired with experience, do you accept that you must continue to be open to learning and growth as you embrace this new responsibility?
Youth:	I do, and I ask God to help and guide me.
Leader:	Many circumstances can compromise your ability to fulfill this commitment: the influence of drugs or alcohol, the distraction of passengers, the inattentiveness of being overly tired, and the temptation to show off among peers are but a few. Do you, therefore, promise to turn away from those things that might impair your ability to drive responsibly?
Youth:	I do, and I ask God to help and guide me.

Leader:	(addressing the youth's family and friends) Responsible driving habits are more readily established with the support of family and friends. Do you promise to support _____ in his/her commitment to safe and responsible driving?
All:	We do, and we ask God to help and guide us.
Leader:	With what symbols shall we mark the significance of this occasion?
Parent(s):	I/we, your parent(s), present you with this set of car keys. With them comes my/our confidence in your ability, my/our hope for your maturity, and my/our prayers for your safety.

The car keys are presented.

Friends:	We, your friends, present you with this key chain. With it comes our encouragement and support for driving safely, responsibly, and courteously.

The key chain is presented.

Leader:	Let us pray.
	Most Gracious God, we seek your blessing for _____ at this time of transition to greater self-accountability. Give him/her clarity of judgment, generosity of spirit, and control of self so that he/she may mature in his/her faithful stewarding of the privileges and responsibilities entrusted to him/her. We pray in the name of your Son, Jesus Christ our Lord, whose love and grace sustain us in all we do.
All:	Amen! May it be so!
Leader:	(addressing the youth) May Almighty God, Father, Son, and Holy Spirit, bless your going out and your coming in from this time on and forevermore!
All:	Amen! Thanks be to God!

| Leader: | The peace of the Lord be with you always! |
| All: | And also with you! |

The rite concludes with a sharing of the peace.

Go in Peace
For a Young Adult Leaving Home

Even among the most independent and adventuresome young adults, departure from home for college, work, or military service can give rise to complex feelings of anxiety and loss. This rite is designed to equip the young adult with the assurances and well wishes of the most significant people in his/her life—assurances and well wishes that, without the ritual marking of this time, might well go unspoken.

This rite may appropriately be incorporated into a gathering of family and close friends, perhaps in conjunction with a celebratory meal. Go over the rite with the parents of the young adult and ensure that they will provide a quilt, blanket, or afghan for presentation during the rite. Recruit a trusted friend or family member (someone other than a parent) to lead the rite. Recruit one or two friends or siblings to read the scripture lessons. So that they may prepare for their respective roles, make copies of the rite available in advance to the parents, leader, and reader(s).

When it is time to begin, invite participants to stand and form a circle around the young adult who is leaving. Make copies of the rite available to all participants.

Leader:	The Lord be with you!
All:	And also with you!

Reader #1:	A reading from Isaiah, chapter forty-three:

Do not fear, for I have redeemed you; I have called you by name, you are mine. When you pass through the waters, I will be with you; and through the rivers, they shall not overwhelm you; when you walk through fire you shall not be burned, and the flame shall not consume you. For I am the Lord your God, the Holy One of Israel, your Savior. (*Isaiah 43:1b–3a*)

The word of the Lord!

All:	Thanks be to God!

Leader:	(*addressing the community*) A young adult's departure from home is a significant event in his/her life and in the lives of his/her family and friends. As _____ prepares to leave home for _____, we gather to mark the significance of his/her leaving.

Leader:	(*addressing young adult*) Are you prepared to leave the familiarity of family and friends in order to begin this important new chapter in your journey to adulthood?
Young Adult:	Yes, by the help of God.

Leader:	We know that you will face opportunities and challenges and that you will experience joys and disappointments. We know that you will encounter new ways, new images, and new models that you will test and learn from. We ask that, in your learning and growing, you will be mindful of the people and experiences that brought you to this crossroads and of the God whose love will journey with you wherever you go.
	Hear now the hopes envisioned for you as you begin this adventure.

As they are moved, participants articulate their hopes and dreams for the young adult. When all have had opportunity to contribute, the rite continues.

Leader:	(*addressing the community*) What symbol will accompany _____ on his/her journey into new experiences?
Parent(s):	This gift represents our assurance that you will be surrounded by our love wherever you go.

The parent(s) place(s) the quilt, blanket, or afghan around the young adult's shoulders.

Leader:	Let us pray.
	Almighty God, be with _____ at this important crossroads in his/her journey into a

future of wondrous possibility. Bless his/her efforts, guide his/her choices, confirm his/her gifts, and support his/her growth, that he/she may faithfully discern your will for his/her life. Be with us that we may appropriately share in his/her joys, support him/her in his/her disappointments, and confidently commend him/her to your loving care. In the name Jesus, your Son and our Savior, who journeys with _____ wherever he/she goes.

All: Amen! May it be so!

Reader #2:   A reading from Acts, chapter thirteen:

"While they were worshiping the Lord and fasting, the Holy Spirit said, 'Set apart for me Barnabas and Saul for the work to which I have called them.' Then after fasting and praying they laid their hands on them and sent them off." *(Acts 13:2–3)*

The word of the Lord!

All: Thanks be to God!

Those gathered may place their hands on the young adult's head and shoulders.

Leader: *(addressing young adult)*
May God bless you and keep you.
May God's face shine on you and be gracious to you.
May God look upon you with favor and give you peace.

All: Amen! Thanks be to God!

Hands are withdrawn.

Leader: The peace of the Lord be with you always!
All: And also with you!

The rite concludes with a sharing of the peace.

The Work of Our Hands
Marking the Beginning of a New Job or Career

Whether a new job or career has been chosen with great intentionality or stumbled into without a great deal of forethought, entrance into that job or career marks a transition into a new way of being. This rite invites reflection on the relationship between God's work in creating the universe and humankind's work in sustaining life.

The rite may appropriately be incorporated into a gathering of family and/or friends, perhaps in conjunction with a celebratory meal. Go over the rite with the individual seeking God's blessing, ensuring that he/she will bring to the rite some tangible symbol of his/her job/career and be prepared to share its significance. Recruit a friend or family member to lead the rite. So that they may have opportunity to prepare for their respective roles, make copies of the rite available in advance to the leader and the individual beginning a new job/career.

When it is time to begin, invite participants to form a circle around the individual. Make copies of the rite available for all participants.

Leader: The Lord be with you!
All: And also with you!

Leader: Lord, you have been our dwelling place in all generations.
All: Before the mountains were brought forth, or ever you had formed the earth and the world, from everlasting to everlasting you are God.

Leader: Let your work be manifest to your servants, and your glorious power to their children.
All: Let the favor of the Lord our God be upon us, and prosper for us the work of our hands—O prosper the work of our hands! *(Psalm 90:1–2,16–17)*

Leader: *(addressing the community)* Every day gives cause to celebrate God's gift of vocation as it unfolds in the work embraced by God's people throughout the world. On this day, we are gathered to ask God's blessing on the future labors of _____ as he/she begins a new job/career.

Leader: *(addressing person beginning new job/career)* What do you hold in your hands as a symbol of your new career?

The person identifies the item and briefly shares its significance as a symbol of his/her future labors.

Leader: *(addressing person beginning new job/career)* Will you extend your hands and this symbol of your future labors to receive God's blessing?.

The leader places his/her hand on the participant's hands.

Leader: May God bless you and keep you.

May God's face shine on you and be gracious to you.

May God look on you with favor and give you peace.

All: Amen! Thanks be to God!

Hands are withdrawn.

Leader: Let us pray.

Creator God, we seek your blessing for _____ as he/she begins this new chapter in a life of service to you. Fill him/her with confidence for stewarding the gifts you have entrusted to him/her and compassion for his/her interactions with others. Inspire in him/her both a commitment to diligent work and a commitment to the practice of self-care, so that he/she may enjoy both the satisfaction of productive work and the rejuvenation of rest from labor and renewal in you. Nurture within him/her such clarity of purpose and integrity of action that all the labors of

All Creatures, Great and Small
Blessing of Pets

Surely, pets are among God's most endearing blessings, offering enrichment, companionship, and joy. This rite offers an opportunity to give thanks for the presence of pets in our lives and to commit ourselves to responsible care of our pets and of God's creation.

This rite is intended for use at a gathering of the community, perhaps near the date when the church commemorates the life and witness of St. Francis of Assisi (October 4). The ideal setting for the rite is a contained out-of-doors area, perhaps a courtyard. A statue of St. Francis of Assisi would provide an appropriate focal point for the rite. For the safety of all, pet owners must keep their pets on a leash or in a container at all times.

Recruit to lead this rite a religious leader who is at ease in front of a group, comfortable interacting with animals, and gifted in responding to the unexpected with grace and flexibility. Alert the leader that some participants may request a blessing for former pets by presenting photos or other memorabilia and that young children may bring toys or stuffed animals to receive a blessing (provision is made in the rite for such occasions). Encourage the leader to greet each participant as he/she arrives with his/her pet, inquiring about the pet's name and expressing an interest in the place the pet has occupied in that person's life. So that he/she may prepare for his/her role, make a copy of the rite available to him/her in advance.

Pet owners will be delighted if a photographer is on hand to record the blessing of their pet. The rite may appropriately conclude with some simple refreshments, perhaps beverages, animal crackers, and a variety of healthful pet treats.

When it is time to begin, invite participants to stand. Make copies of the rite available for all participants.

| Leader: | The Lord be with you! |
| All: | And also with you! |

| Leader: | O Lord, how manifold are your works! |
| All: | You stretch out the heavens like a tent. You set the |

his/her hands and heart may be expressive of loving intentions for all people. We pray in the n of your Son, Jesus Christ our Lord, whose l makes us one in you.

All: Amen! May it be so!

Leader: The peace of the Lord be with you always!
All: And also with you!

The rite concludes with a sharing of the peace.

earth on its foundations. You make springs gush forth in the valleys and give drink to every animal.

Leader: You plant trees where birds may build their nests.
All: You cause the grass to grow for the cattle and plants for people to use. You open your hand and give all creatures their food in good season.
(Psalm 104:2, 5, 10–11, 14, 17, 24, 27–28)

Leader: *(addressing the community)* We have come together to acknowledge with gratitude the goodness of God in all creatures, great and small, and to seek God's blessing on the pets that are our companions in life.

Let us pray.

On this day, O God, we offer thanks for these, our pets, who are your daily instruments of joy and comfort in our lives. Even as you demonstrate care for us, so also move us to demonstrate care for these and all your creatures, knowing that, in so doing, we are privileged to share in your love of creation. We pray in the name of Jesus, in whose power we are made a new creation,

All: Amen! May it be so!

As the leader approaches each pet, the pet's owner speaks the pet's name aloud so that all those gathered may hear. The leader then raises his/her hand above the pet and speaks a word of blessing.

Leader: May God Creator bless you and keep you through all the days of your life!
All: *(after each blessing)* Thanks be to God!

If some participants have brought mementos of former pets, the leader may touch each memento, while speaking these or similar words.

Leader: May God bless the memory of this pet's presence in your life!

All: Thanks be to God!

If children have brought stuffed animals to receive a blessing, the leader may touch each toy, while speaking these or similar words.

Leader: May this animal's presence be a source of joy and comfort in this child's life!
All: Thanks be to God!

When the time of blessing is concluded, the rite continues.

Leader: May God Almighty, Father, Son, and Holy Spirit, use us as instruments of blessing for all creatures, great and small!
All: Amen! Thanks be to God!

Leader: The peace of the Lord be with you always!
All: And also with you!

The rite concludes with a sharing of the peace,
which may be followed by a time of fellowship and refreshment.

The Seventh Day
Marking Retirement from One's Life Work

Retirement from one's life work signals a significant life passage. This rite is designed to honor the significance of this event as an ending, while locating the event within the larger context of a new beginning—a transition to new hopes, plans, and experiences.

This rite is intended for use within a circle of close friends and family members, perhaps in conjunction with a celebratory meal. It would, however, be best not to try to incorporate this ritual into a retirement party, where the tone of the gathering would not likely be conducive to the kind of mindful reflection that this rite invites.

To prepare for this rite, consider assembling a simple display of mementos that represent the life work of the one retiring. For some, that might mean computer diskettes and program flowcharts; for others, it might mean a hard hat and blueprints or construction tools; for yet others, it might mean a diner menu and order pad. Be creative in considering what items might best represent this individual's investment of self through work.

Recruit a friend or family member to lead the rite. Enlist the help of the retiring individual and his/her family and friends in preparing a succinct summary of his/her life work. Recruit several people to collaborate in the selection of an item or items to mark the significance of the individual's retirement—perhaps an item drawn from the display (see above) that affirms the contributions the individual has made through his/her life work, and ensure that someone is prepared to present it and offer a few brief words. Go over the rite with the retiring individual and ensure that he/she will come prepared to share an item that conveys his/her hopes and/or plans for this new chapter in his/her life. In both instances, explain that items prompting thoughtful reflection are preferable to plaques, certificates, or items of high material value. So that they may have opportunity to prepare for their respective roles, make copies of the rite available in advance to the leader, presenters, and retiree.

When it is time to begin, invite participants to stand.

Make copies of the rite available for all participants.

| Leader: | The Lord be with you! |
| All: | And also with you! |

| Reader: | Lord, you have been our dwelling place in all generations. |
| All: | Before the mountains were brought forth, or ever you had formed the earth and the world, from everlasting to everlasting you are God. |

| Reader: | A thousand years in your sight are like yesterday when it is past. |
| All: | You sweep the years away; they are like a dream. |

| Reader: | Teach us to count our days so that we may gain a wise heart. |
| All: | Satisfy us in the morning with your steadfast love, so that we may rejoice and be glad all our days. |

| Reader: | Let your work be manifest to your servants, and your glorious power to their children. |
| All: | Let the favor of the Lord our God be upon us, and prosper for us the work of our hands. *(Psalm 90:1–2, 4–5, 12, 14, 16–17)* |

| Leader: | *(addressing the community)* We read in the book of Genesis about the six days of God's labor in creating the universe and about the seventh day, when creation was complete and God enjoyed a time of rest and rejuvenation. |

Today, we gather to celebrate another completion of labor, one that is signaled by _____'s retirement from his/her life work. Of what has this life of labor consisted?

Time is allowed for a brief summary or description of the retiring individual's life work to be shared. When the sharing has concluded, the rite continues.

Leader: (*addressing the retiring individual*) Your life work is indeed a cause for celebration! "Therefore, . . . be steadfast, immovable, always excelling in the work of the Lord, because you know that in the Lord your labor is not in vain." (*I Corinthians 15:58*)

(*addressing the community*) With what shall we mark the completion of _____'s life work?

Time is allowed for a presentation by family and friends. When the presentation has concluded, the rite continues.

Leader: (*addressing the retiring individual*) Even as God's labor did not end with completion of the world's creation, so also does your labor not end with completion of your life work. Your retirement signals the completion of one chapter and the beginning of another; it marks your entrance into a time of greater freedom for rest, recreation, and pursuit of those activities that bring you joy. With what will you mark this beginning of your seventh day?

Time is allowed for the retiree to share a symbol of his/her hopes and/or plans for his/her retirement. When the sharing has concluded, the rite continues.

Leader: Let us pray.

Direct us, O God, so that all our doings—begun, continued, and ended in you—may bring glory to your holy name. Guide young people facing difficult choices about their life's work. Support those laboring faithfully, contributing to the good of all. Encourage those who are underemployed or facing a time of unemployment. On this day, we especially ask your blessing of _____, who, in having completed his/her life's work, now begins his/her celebration of a seventh day, both as a time of rest and recreation and as a time of renewed life and service.

All:	Amen! May it be so!

Leader:	*(addressing the retiring individual)*
	May God bless you and keep you!
	May God's face shine on you and be gracious to you!
	May God look on you with favor and give you peace!
All:	Amen! Thanks be to God!

Leader:	The peace of the Lord be with you always!
All:	And also with you!

The rite concludes with a sharing of the peace.

Measure of Our Days
Marking the Preparation of a Will

Preparation of a will is one way to bring mindful closure to the life-long responsibility for stewarding God's gifts and blessings. As with any other major decision, the decisions that give shape to one's last will and testament ought to reflect prayerful discernment of God's will.

This rite is designed to engender prayer support in that discernment process. In the rite, participants are invited into heightened awareness of the divine origination of all blessings, the temporality of human existence, and the responsibility of each person to steward the blessings of his/her life to the glory of God and the well-being of others.

The rite is intended for use among a small circle of close family and friends who have the capacity to provide the support being sought and is most appropriately used when a group has been assembled for this express purpose. Recruit one friend or family member to lead the rite and another to read the scripture lesson. So that they may have opportunity to prepare for their respective roles, make copies of the rite available in advance to the leader, reader, and the person(s) seeking support for discernment.

When it is time to begin, invite participants to be seated in a circle. Make copies of the rite available to all participants.

Leader:	The Lord be with you!
All:	And also with you!

Leader:	Lord, let me know my end, and what is the measure of my days; let me know how fleeting my life is,
All:	for I am your passing guest, an alien, like all my forebears.

Leader:	You have made my days a few handbreadths, and my lifetime is as nothing in your sight.
All:	Surely everyone stands as a mere breath. Surely everyone goes about like a shadow.

Leader:	Surely for nothing they are in turmoil; they heap up and do not know who will gather.
All:	O Lord, what do I wait for? My hope is in you! *(Psalm 39:4–5, 7, 12)*
Reader:	A reading from the first letter of Peter, the fourth chapter:

Since therefore Christ suffered in the flesh, arm yourselves also with the same intention, so as to live for the rest of your earthly life no longer by human desires but by the will of God. Maintain constant love for one another. . . . Be hospitable to one another without complaining. Like good stewards of the manifold grace of God, serve one another with whatever gift each of you has received. Whoever speaks must do so as one speaking the very words of God; whoever serves must do so with the strength that God supplies, so that God may be glorified in all things through Jesus Christ.
(I Peter 4:1–2, 8–11)

The word of the Lord!

All:	Thanks be to God!
Leader:	*(addressing the community)* Throughout the measure of our days, we are entrusted by God with many blessings. Daily, we are called to faithfully steward those blessings through lives of gratitude to God and generosity to others.

One aspect of our stewardship is arranging for mindful distribution of God's blessings at the time of our death. In the desire to be faithful caretaker(s) of what God has entrusted to him/her/them, _____ has/have entered into the process of preparing a will. He/she/they has/have requested our support in prayerfully discerning God's will in the formulation of this last will and testament.

Will you support _____ in his/her/their prayerful discernment?

Participants: We will, and we ask God to help and guide us.

Leader: *(addressing the person[s] preparing a will)* Are there particular concerns that you will entrust to your partners in prayer?

If desired, time is allowed for a brief sharing of concerns. When the sharing concludes, the rite continues.

Leader: Alpha and Omega, the beginning and ending of all our days, we will be still, so that we may know that you are God!

Several minutes are allowed for silent reflection and prayer. At the conclusion of that time, the rite continues.

Leader: *(addressing the community)* What insights will you share to aid in _____'s discernment?

Time is allowed for a brief sharing of insights and words of encouragement. When the time of sharing has concluded, the rite continues.

Leader: Let us pray.

Good and gracious God, we praise you for the abundance of your blessing, known to us in your gifts of time, talent, and treasure. Empower us, we pray, to be faithful stewards of your goodness so that,

All: In life and in death, God may be glorified!

Leader: Good and gracious God, we praise you for the abundance of your blessing in the life/lives of _____. Empower him/her/them, we pray, to be faithful steward(s) of your goodness so that,

All: In life and in death, God may be glorified!

Leader:	Good and gracious God, we praise you for the fullness of your blessing in sending your Son, Jesus Christ our Lord, to claim for us the promise of eternal life in you. Empower us, we pray, to be faithful stewards of your grace, so that,
All:	In life and in death, God may be glorified!
Leader:	In the lives we lead and legacies we leave,
All:	May all glory and honor be yours, O God, now and forever! Amen!
Leader:	May God bless us and keep us,
All:	That the measure of our days may be many!
Leader:	May the Lord's face shine on us and be gracious to us,
All:	That the measure of our days may be fruitful!
Leader:	May the Lord look upon us with favor and give us peace,
All:	That the measure of our days may give glory to God!
Leader:	The peace of the Lord be with you always!
All:	And also with you!

The rite concludes with a sharing of the peace.

III

ENCOURAGEMENT

Wait for the Lord
Marking Entrance into Labor

Most women enter into labor feeling both eagerness for their baby to be born and dread for what the birthing process may be like. This rite validates the significance of those emotions while cultivating mindful appreciation of God's role in sustaining the mother and protecting the baby.

Obviously, not all births lend themselves to the incorporation of ritual as the woman begins labor, but some do. This brief rite is intended for use after the expectant mother has arrived and is settled at the birthing site. It may be used either to shape a prayerful moment between the expectant mother and her partner or birthing coach or to create a reflective moment within a broader circle that might include medical personnel and/or family members on hand to await the birth.

Well in advance of the birth, share a copy of the rite with the expectant parents and invite them to discern whether they think it could be a helpful element in their preparation for the birthing process. If they believe the rite could be helpful to them, recruit a trusted friend or family member to lead the rite and prepare copies of the rite so they are ready when the expectant mother enters into labor.

It is, of course, impossible to know in advance whether, once labor has begun, the expectant parents will have either the time or the inclination to actually make use of the rite. Gift them with the flexibility to use or not use the rite, depending on their in-the-moment experiences of the birthing process.

When it is time to begin, invite participants to form a circle around the expectant mother. Make copies of the rite available to all participants.

Leader: The Lord be with you!
All: And also with you!

Leader: Be strong, and let your heart take courage.
All: Wait for the Lord!

Leader:	The Lord is my light and my salvation; whom shall I fear?
All:	The Lord is the stronghold of my life; of what shall I be afraid?
Leader:	Hear, O Lord, when I cry aloud.
All:	Be gracious to me and answer me!
Leader:	Be strong, and let your heart take courage.
All:	Wait for the Lord! *(Psalm 27:1–2, 7, 14)*
Leader:	*(addressing the community)* The Apostle Paul frequently offered the image of a woman in the throes of labor as a source of encouragement during times of suffering. Labor pains, Paul emphasized, are purposed in the delivery of new life, in the eventual realization of great joy.

As _____ enters into the hard work of labor, she will be sustained by her vision of that purpose—bringing to birth the new life that she has carried and cared for throughout these months of her pregnancy.

Those present join hands, encircling the expectant mother.

Leader:	Let us pray.

O Lord our God, creator of all that was, is, and yet may be, we thank you for the privilege of witnessing this unfolding of your creative work. Protect and sustain _____ during this birthing of new life and call forth this new life in health and wholeness. Prepare the hearts and lives of this/these expectant parent(s) that she/they may welcome this new life with gratitude, affection, and commitment. In the name of Jesus Christ our Lord, we pray,

All:	Amen.

The leader places his/her hand on the expectant mother's head or on the expectant couple's joined hands.

Leader: May God bless you and keep you!
                 May God's face shine on you and be gracious to you!
                 May God look on you with favor and give you peace!
All: Amen! May it be so!

The leader's hand is withdrawn.

Leader: The Lord be with you.
All: And also with you.

The rite concludes with a sharing of the peace.

In the Fullness of Time
Marking Entrance into the Adoption Process

The decision to seek adoption of a child marks entrance into a process that can leave prospective parents vulnerable to painful cycles of hopefulness and despair. This rite grounds the highs and lows of the adoption process within the larger context of God's will unfolding among prospective parents, birth parents, children in need of loving homes, and others playing roles in the adoption process.

The rite is intended for use within an intimate circle of close family and friends, persons who can be relied upon to provide a network of prayer and support as the prospective parent(s) negotiate his/her/their way through the adoption process. It may appropriately be held in conjunction with a meal or other gathering.

Go over the rite with the prospective parent(s) in advance. Recruit one friend or family member to lead the rite and one (or two) other friends or family members to read the brief scripture lessons. In order that they may prepare for their respective roles, make copies of the rite available in advance to the leader, reader(s), and prospective parent(s).

When it is time to begin, invite participants to be seated informally, in a circle. Make copies of the rite available for all participants.

Leader:	The Lord be with you!
All:	And also with you!
Leader:	O God, do not be far away; come quickly to my aid!
All:	It was you who took me from the womb; you kept me safe on my mother's breast.
Leader:	On you I was cast from my birth, and since my mother bore me you have been my God.
All:	O God, do not be far away; come quickly to my aid! *(Psalm 22:9–10, 19)*
Reader #1:	A reading from St. Paul's letter to the Ephesians, the first chapter:

Blessed be the God and Father of our Lord Jesus Christ, who has blessed us in Christ with every spiritual blessing ... [even] as he chose us in Christ before the foundation of the world to be holy and blameless before him in love. He destined us for adoption as his children through Jesus Christ, according to the good pleasure of his will, to the praise of his glorious grace that he freely bestowed on us in the Beloved. In him we have redemption through his blood, the forgiveness of our trespasses, according to the riches of his grace that he lavished on us. With all wisdom and insight he has made known to us the mystery of his will, according to his good pleasure that he set forth in Christ, as a plan for the fullness of time, to gather up all things in him, things in heaven and things on earth. In Christ we have also obtained an inheritance, having been destined according to the purpose of him who accomplishes all things according to his counsel and will, so that we, who were the first to set our hope on Christ, might live for the praise of his glory. (*Ephesians 1:3–12*)

The word of the Lord!

All: Thanks be to God!

Reader #2: A reading from the gospel according to John, the fourteenth chapter:

And Jesus said, "I will not leave you orphaned; I am coming to you. In a little while the world will no longer see me, but you will see me; because I live, you also will live. On that day you will know that I am in my Father, and you in me, and I in you. Those who love me will keep my word, and my Father will love them, and we will come to them and make our home with them.

"Peace I leave with you; my peace I give you . . . Do not let your hearts be troubled, and do not let them be afraid." (*John 14:18–20, 23, 27*)

The gospel of the Lord!

All: Thanks be to God!

Leader: We are gathered together to seek the blessing of God on _____'s decision to enter into the process for adopting a child. We do so knowing that his/her/their progress in this process may hold challenges, that he/she/they may well experience times of struggle and frustration, and that his/her/their hope for a child may be fulfilled quickly, slowly, or not at all.

Let us pray.

Divine Parent, we know that it is your will for all children to be received into loving homes and hearts. Draw near to _____ as he/she/they prepare a place of welcome for a child, that this period of anticipation may be a time of growth in knowledge of self and faith in you. God of mercy,

All: In the fullness of time, may the mystery of your will unfold.

Leader: Draw near to all those who play roles in the adoption process, that they may exercise insight in their discernments, compassion in their judgments, and wisdom in their decisions. God of mercy,

All: In the fullness of time, may the mystery of your will unfold.

Leader: Draw near to birth parents facing difficult choices about their parenting responsibilities, that they may have the courage to make decisions that honor the best interests of their children. God of mercy,

All: In the fullness of time, may the mystery of your will unfold.

Leader: Draw near to children in need of loving homes, that they may know the comfort of your presence, the safety of your protection, and the joy of timely placement with loving parents. God of mercy,

All: In the fullness of time, may the mystery of your will unfold.

Leader: O God, we know that like a mother you long to gather us to yourself and like a father you yearn to welcome us into the arms of your love. Gather _____ into your wide embrace and hold him/her/them securely in your love, that he/she/they may be sustained in his/her/their journey and at peace with the unfolding mystery of your will for him/her/them.

All: We pray in the name of Christ, through whom you have adopted us as your own, Amen.

Leader: In the riches of God's abundant grace,
All: May God bless us and keep us!

Leader: In God's plan for the fullness of time,
All: May God's face shine on us and be gracious to us!

Leader: In the mysterious unfolding of God's will,
All: May God look on us with favor and give us peace!

Leader: The peace of the Lord be with you always!
All: And also with you!

The rite concludes with a sharing of the peace.

Let Your Heart Take Courage
Seeking God's Will and Direction

Sometimes God's guidance seems clear; at other times we struggle to discern God's will and direction. This rite, intended for those times when the path through the wilderness of choice and direction is unclear, appropriately enlists the counsel and prayer support of Christian brothers and sisters to aid in discernment of God's will.

The rite is suitable for use within the family circle or in conjunction with a Bible study or prayer meeting, a small group ministry gathering, a church youth group session, or some other small assembly of faith partners. Recruit one person to lead the rite and another to read the brief scripture lesson. So that they may have opportunity to prepare for their respective roles, make copies of the rite available in advance to the leader, reader, and person seeking support for his/her discernment.

To prepare for the rite, place a candle and an open Bible in a prominent place in the room where the rite is being held. When it is time for the rite to begin, light the candle and invite those gathered to be seated informally in a circle (either in chairs or on the floor or ground). Make copies of the rite available to all participants.

Leader: The Lord be with you!
All: And also with you!

Reader: A reading from Isaiah, the forty-third chapter:

Thus says the Lord, he who created you . . . [and] formed you . . . : Do not fear, for I have redeemed you; I have called you by name, you are mine. I will make a way in the wilderness and rivers in the desert. For I am the Lord your God, . . . [and] you are precious in my sight. *(Isaiah 43:1, 3–4, 19)*

The word of the Lord!

All: Thanks be to God!

| Leader: | The Lord will guide you continually, and satisfy your needs in parched places. |
| All: | Wait for the Lord; be strong, and let your heart take courage! |

| Leader: | Surely I know the plans I have for you, says the Lord, plans for your welfare and not for harm, to give you a future with hope. |
| All: | Wait for the Lord; be strong, and let your heart take courage! |

| Leader: | My heart is glad, and my soul rejoices, . . . for you show me the path of life. |
| All: | Wait for the Lord; be strong, and let your heart take courage! |

| Leader: | You shall be like a watered garden, like a spring whose waters never fail. (*Isaiah 58:116*) |
| All: | Wait for the Lord; be strong, and let your heart take courage! (*Psalm 16:9, 11; 27:14; Isaiah 58:11; Jeremiah 29:11*) |

| Leader: | (*addressing the community*) Discernment of God's will is the privilege and challenge of all who follow in the way of Christ. Whether confronted by too many options, by inadequate options, or by the inability to perceive the options available to us, there are times when it is appropriate to enlist the counsel and prayer support of Christian brothers and sisters to aid us in our discernment. |

We gather in this place as partners with _____ in his/her discernment of God's direction for his/her life.

(*addressing individual seeking direction*) _____, for what aspects of your life do you seek particular guidance at this time?

Time is allowed for a brief elaboration of concerns. When the time of sharing has concluded, the rite continues.

Leader: We join our hearts as one in discerning God's will for

            _____.

Time is allowed for silent prayers for discernment. After a period of several minutes, the rite continues.

Leader: *(addressing the community)* What insights will we offer to aid _____ in his/her discernment and decision making?

Time is allowed for brief sharing.

Leader: Let us pray.

            God of all that was, is, and yet shall be, make your will known to _____. Assure him/her of the certainty of your love. Open his/her heart to the possibilities you have fashioned for him/her. Replace his/her uncertainty with confidence. Transform his/her confusion into clarity of direction and purpose. Bless his/her choices and give him/her courage to trust your promise that all things work together for good to those who love you.

All: We pray in the name of Christ, who is for us the way, the truth, and the light, Amen.

Leader: *(addressing the person seeking God's direction)* Let your heart take courage,
All: For God will bless you and keep you!

Leader: Let your heart take courage,
All: For God's face will shine on you and be gracious to you!

Leader:	Let your heart take courage,
All:	For God will look on you with favor and give you peace!

Leader:	The peace of the Lord be with you always!
All:	And also with you!

The rite concludes with a sharing of the peace.

Can These Bones Live?
Times of Unemployment or Underemployment

Extended periods of unemployment or underemployment can set in motion a debilitating cycle of despair. Unable to find suitable employment, one becomes discouraged and begins to question one's abilities. Lacking confidence, one is unable to take full advantage of the opportunities that are available and so becomes even more discouraged. This rite offers one way for Christian brothers and sisters to offer support and encouragement during such difficult times.

The rite is intended for use within a small circle of close friends and/or family. It may appropriately be used in conjunction with an informal gathering of persons whose history has included a willingness to support one another in prayer. Be mindful that the unemployed/underemployed individual may be too discouraged to recognize his/her need for support or too embarrassed to ask for it, so the initiative for making use of this rite may need to come from someone else.

Go over the rite with the unemployed/underemployed individual to determine his/her willingness to participate and to discuss his/her role in it. Recruit one friend or family member to lead the rite and another to read the scripture lesson. So that they may have an opportunity to prepare for their respective roles, make copies of the rite available in advance to the leader, reader, and unemployed/underemployed individual.

To prepare for the rite, assemble some items to characterize the individual's discouragement (such as his/her resume, newspaper want ads, a file of rejection letters, and so forth.) and arrange them on a small table with a candle and cross or open Bible. When it is time to begin, light the candle and invite participants to be seated in a circle in close proximity to the items. Make copies of the rite available to all participants.

Leader:	The Lord be with you!
All:	And also with you!
Leader:	To you, O Lord, I lift up my soul.
All:	Renew the strength of those who wait for you!

Leader:	Turn to me, [O Lord,] and be gracious to me.
All:	Make me to know your ways, O Lord; teach me your paths.
Leader:	O guard my life, and deliver me, . . . for I take refuge in you;
All:	Relieve the troubles of my heart, and bring me out of my distress.
Leader:	To you, O Lord, I lift up my soul.
All:	Renew the strength of those who wait for you!
	(Psalm 25:, 4, 16a, 17, 20; Isaiah 40:1)
Reader:	A reading from Ezekiel, the thirty-seventh chapter:

The hand of the Lord came upon me, and he brought me out by the spirit of the Lord and set me down in the middle of a valley; it was full of bones. He led me all around them; there were very many lying in the valley, and they were very dry. He said to me, "Mortal, can these bones live?" I answered, "O Lord God, you know." Then he said to me, "Prophesy to these bones, and say to them: O dry bones, hear the word of the Lord. Thus says the Lord God to these bones: I will cause breath to enter you, and you shall live. I will lay sinews on you, and will cause flesh to come upon you, and cover you with skin, and put breath in you, and you shall live; and you shall know that I am the Lord."

So I prophesied as I had been commanded; and as I prophesied, suddenly there was a noise, a rattling, and the bones came together, bone to its bone. I looked, and there were sinews on them, and flesh had come upon them, and skin had covered them; but there was no breath in them. Then he said to me, "Prophesy to the breath, prophesy, mortal, and say to the breath: Thus says the Lord God: Come from the four winds, O breath, and breathe upon these slain, that they may live." I prophesied as he commanded

me, and the breath came into them, and they lived, and stood on their feet, a vast multitude.
(Ezekiel 37:1–10)

The word of the Lord!

All: Thanks be to God!

Leader: *(addressing the community)* In the labors of our lives, we are privileged to participate in God's ongoing work of creation. Being denied that privilege can leave us feeling discouraged, empty, like there is no life left in us.

We are gathered to acknowledge that ＿＿＿＿＿＿ is in such a place of discouragement and emptiness. We have come together to offer support and encouragement through our witness to God's ability to call forth life from even the most desolate places of our lives.

(addressing the one who is unemployed or underemployed) ＿＿＿＿＿＿, what will you share with us of your discouragement?

The unemployed or underemployed person may briefly describe his/her situation and the nature of the discouragement he/she is experiencing. When the sharing has concluded, the rite continues.

Leader: Let us pray.

We praise you, O God, for the privilege of laboring in partnership with you and in service to others. Make your presence known, we pray, among employers and employees, that they may share life-giving partnerships and produce God-pleasing goods and services. Whenever abusive attitudes and practices cause them to question whether "these bones" can live,

All: Renew them with your breath of life!

| Leader: | We praise you, O God, for the wondrous diversity of talents and abilities that you have entrusted to each of us. Make your presence known, we pray, to those for whom unemployment or underemployment prevent full expression of those gifts. Whenever discouragement in the search for fulfilling employment leads us to question whether "these bones" can live, |
| All: | Renew us with your breath of life! |

| Leader: | We praise you, O God, for _____'s longing to steward well the personal resources you have entrusted to him/her. Make your presence known, we pray, in his/her search for employment that is both challenging and gratifying. Whenever the pace of his/her progress causes him/her to question whether "these bones" can live, |
| All: | Renew him/her with your breath of life! |

| Leader: | In these and in all things, O God, give us courage to entrust the cares of our hearts to you, knowing that you are working all things together for the good of those who love you. In the name of Christ, we pray, |
| All: | Amen! May it be so! |

Participants may gather in a circle around the unemployed/underemployed individual and place their hands on his/her shoulders.

Leader:	*(addressing the unemployed/underemployed person)*
	May God bless you and keep you in your search for meaningful work!
	May God's face shine on you and be gracious to you as you prayerfully steward the gifts and opportunities available to you!
	May God look on you with favor and give you peace as God calls forth in you new life!
All:	Amen! Thanks be to God!

Hands are withdrawn.

Leader: The peace of the Lord be with you always!
All: And also with you!

The rite concludes with a sharing of the peace.

Wherever You Go
Farewell

In a culture in which geographic relocations are common, one's circle of friends may frequently undergo dramatic change. Whether we are the one leaving or the one being left, we long to achieve closure of those relationships in ways that affirm their significance. This rite creates space to acknowledge the grief that is ingredient to leaving and being left, as well as opportunity to name what has been cherished in the relationship.

This rite is intended for use within a circle of friends who have shared a special bond with each other. It may appropriately be used in conjunction with a special farewell dinner or other gathering.

Recruit someone from within the circle to lead the rite and invite him/her to familiarize himself/herself with his/her leadership role. Alert participants that the rite will afford opportunity to affirm what they have especially treasured in the relationships they have been privileged to share.

When it is time to begin, invite participants to gather in a circle. Make copies of the rite available to all participants.

Leader: The Lord be with you!
All: And also with you!

Leader: I lift up my eyes to the hills—from where will my help come?
All: My help comes from the Lord, who made heaven and earth.

Leader: He will not allow your foot to be moved: he who keeps you will not slumber.
All: He who keeps Israel will neither slumber nor sleep.

Leader: The Lord is your keeper; the Lord is your shade at your right hand.
All: The sun shall not strike you by day, nor the moon by night.

| Leader: | The Lord will keep you from all evil, he will keep your life. |
| All: | The Lord will keep your going out and your coming in, from this time on and forevermore. *(Psalm 121)* |

| Leader: | *(addressing the community)* We have gathered in this place to mark the departure of _____ for life in _____. What would we like him/her/them to know in his/her/their leaving? |
| Those Remaining: | *(addressing the one[s] leaving)* God has called you to a new place and a new task. We grieve your leaving! We will miss you! |

Those remaining, as they are moved to do so, may briefly name something they will especially miss. When the sharing has concluded, the rite continues.

| Leader: | *(addressing the one[s] leaving)* What would you like us to know in your leaving? |
| The One(s) Leaving: | *(addressing the ones remaining)* Even though it is time to move to a new place and a new task, I/we will miss the fellowship I/we have shared with you. It is hard to leave! |

The one(s) leaving, if desired, may briefly name what has been especially valued in the relationship. When the sharing has concluded, the rite continues.

| Leader: | Let us pray. |
| | Lord God, you give us as gifts to each other to be treasured, shared, and passed on. Both in our gratitude for what has been and in our hope for what is yet to be, we celebrate the movement of your Spirit among us, continually forming and reforming us. Make your presence known to _____, that he/she/they may find in you refuge for the jour- |

ney, shade from the heat of the day, shelter from the storms of life, rest from the weariness of labor, and protection in times of trouble. So also, make your presence known to us who remain in this place, that we may be comforted by the certain knowledge that, even in our geographic separation, your love will bind us together as members of your family.

All: We claim the promise of your Son, Jesus the Christ, that he will never leave us or forsake us. Amen.

Those Remaining: Lord God, you have called your servants to ventures of which we cannot see the ending, by paths as yet untrodden, through perils unknown.

Those Leaving: Give us faith to go out with good courage, not knowing where we go, but only that your hand is leading us and your love supporting us.

All: Through Jesus Christ our Lord, Amen.
(Adapted from *Lutheran Book of Worship*, 153.)

Those remaining may place their hands on the shoulders of the one(s) leaving.

Leader: May God be with you in your leaving and in your returning, from this time forward and forevermore.

Hands are withdrawn.

Leader: The peace of the Lord be with you always!
All: And also with you!

The rite concludes with a sharing of the peace.

A Clean Heart
Confession of Wrongdoing

Although the Order for Confession and Forgiveness is a common element of public worship for many Christian traditions, confession of specific wrongdoing has, for the most part, become a private matter between the penitent and God. While this practice affirms the Christian belief that, in Christ, we each have unrestricted access to God, it also serves to negate the reality that our wrongdoing often impacts others.

This rite is intended for those situations where the consequences of someone's wrongdoing has harmed the Christian community. It is designed to offer individuals guilty of such wrongdoing an opportunity (1) to confess his/her sin, (2) to demonstrate empathy for the pain of those affected by his/her actions, (3) to declare his/her intentions to amend his/her behavior and, where possible, to make restitution for it, and (4) to pledge renewed commitment to a life of faith. It is further designed to offer the Christian community an opportunity, in hearing the penitent's confession, to absolve the wrongdoer so that, together, they may begin the tough work of rebuilding the community.

Please note that this rite is not intended as a shortcut to "cheap grace." It ought to be considered only after the penitent has experienced genuine remorse, received assurance of God's love and forgiveness, and begun to seek ways to make right his/her wrong—normally through work with his/her pastor or priest. Exercise care to ensure no one feels coerced into participating in the rite.

Because sin is the common context for all human frailty, the temptation is great to fashion this rite as a reciprocal experience. Although situations exist within the community's life when such mutuality is appropriate and desirable, this particular rite is not well suited to them. This rite speaks specifically to those situations where an individual's actions have harmed others and inflicted pain on the community, situations where a clear need exists for the wrongdoer to confess, ask, and receive, and for the community to listen, forgive, and restore.

The faith community's worship space is the ideal setting for this rite. It is expected that the gathering will be small and that participants will assemble in close proximity to one another (perhaps adjacent to the baptismal font or around the eucharistic table). The leader is most appropriately that pastor or priest who has worked with the penitent. Recruit another recognized leader of the faith community to read the scripture lesson. So that they may adequately prepare for their respective roles, make copies of the rite available in advance to the leader, reader, and penitent.

Prepare for the rite by arranging the space in a way that will permit eye contact between the penitent and the gathered community. Subdued lighting will help to create a space conducive to reflection. Lighted candles will signal the presence of God. Water (in the baptismal font or in a small bowl) will provide a reminder of our baptisms, by which we are cleansed of our sin and initiated into Christian community. Make copies of the rite available to all participants.

Leader: In the name of the Father and of the Son and of the Holy Spirit.

All: Amen.

Reader: A reading from the gospel according to Matthew, the ninth chapter:

As Jesus was walking along, he saw a man called Matthew sitting at the tax booth; and he said to him, "Follow me." And he got up and followed him.

And as he sat at dinner in the house, many tax collectors and sinners came and were sitting with him and his disciples. When the Pharisees saw this, they said to his disciples, "Why does your teacher eat with tax collectors and sinners?" But when he heard this, he said, "Those who are well have no need of a physician, but those who are sick. Go and learn what this means, 'I desire mercy, not sacrifice.' For I have come to call not the righteous but sinners."
(Matthew 9:9–13)

The gospel of the Lord!

All: Thanks be to God!

Leader:	*(addressing the community)* The disease of sin is not experienced in isolation; it often damages relationships and injures others. Acknowledging the communal impact of sin, _____ has requested an opportunity to confess his/her wrongdoing within this circle of those who have been hurt by his/her actions.
	(addressing the penitent) _____, are you prepared to make your confession?
Penitent:	I am, and I ask God to help and guide me.
Leader:	*(addressing the community)* Are you prepared to hear _____'s confession?
All:	We are, and we ask God to help and guide us.
Leader:	*(addressing penitent)* Our hearts are open to hear your confession.
Penitent:	*(addressing the community)* Even as I have confessed before God, I now confess to you, my brothers and sisters in Christ, that I am guilty of wrongdoing . . .

Time is allowed for the penitent to confess his/her wrongdoing, to demonstrate empathy for those injured by his/her wrongdoing, to declare his/her intentions for making amends and/or restitution, and to pledge renewed commitment to a life of faithfulness.

When the penitent's confession is concluded, the rite continues.

Penitent:	Create in me a clean heart, O God, and put a new and right spirit within me. Do not cast me away from your presence, and do not take your Holy Spirit from me. Wash me thoroughly from my iniquity, and cleanse me from my sin. Restore to me the joy of your salvation, and sustain in me a willing spirit. *(Psalm 51:2, 10–12)*

All:
The Lord is merciful and gracious,
slow to anger and abounding in steadfast love.
He does not deal with us according to our sins,
nor repay us according to our iniquities.
For as the heavens are high above the earth,
so is his steadfast love
toward those who fear him.
As a father has compassion for his children
so the Lord has compassion for those who fear him.
(Psalm 103:8, 10–13)

Leader:
(addressing the penitent) _____,
what do you ask of this community?

Penitent:
(addressing the community) I ask that you have mercy
according to God's loving kindness and that, in compassion, you forgive my wrongdoing.

Leader:
(addressing the community) You have heard
_____'s confession. As those made
alive in God's grace, will you now affirm the abundance of God's mercy by restoring him/her to this
community of faith?

All:
(addressing the penitent) In obedience to the command of our Lord Jesus Christ, we forgive your
wrongdoing. With joy, we welcome you as a fellow
member of the body of Christ, as a child of the same
Heavenly Father, and as a worker with us in the kingdom of God.
(Inspired by *Lutheran Book of Worship*, 125.)

*The penitent steps into the center of the community. Encircling the pen-
itent, members of the community may place their hands on his/her
shoulders.*

Leader:
God, the Father of our Lord Jesus Christ, we give you
thanks for freeing your sons and daughters from the
power of sin and for raising them up to new life in
you. Pour your Holy Spirit on _____:
the spirit of wisdom and understanding, the spirit of
counsel and might, the spirit of knowledge and the

fear of the Lord, the spirit of joy in your presence. (Inspired by *Lutheran Book of Worship*,124.)

All: Amen! Thanks be to God!

Hands are withdrawn.

Leader: Let us pray.

O God, from whom come all holy desires, all good counsels, and all just works: give to your servant _____ that peace which the world cannot give, that his/her heart may be set free to obey your commandments. Unite our desires into one holy will so that, together, we may faithfully serve you and joyfully care for one another and your creation. In the name of your Son, Jesus Christ our Lord, (Adapted from *Lutheran Book of Worship*, 195.)

All: Amen.

Leader: Blessed are those whose sins have been forgiven, whose wrongdoings have been forgotten!

All: Thanks be to God!

Leader: The peace of the Lord be with you always!

All: And also with you!

The rite concludes with a sharing of the peace.

From This Day Forward
Marking the Dissolution of a Marriage

We know that God intends for the marriage between a man and a woman to be intimate, joyful, and enduring. We also know that, because of our human frailties, God's vision of goodness cannot always be realized. On occasion, we must admit our inability to embrace what we promised and to honor what we intended.

The demise of a marriage should never be taken lightly. However, once a couple reaches a decision to dissolve their union, the energy of the Christian community is appropriately directed to helping the couple achieve God-pleasing closure to their relationship. By seeking to honor what has been, while at the same time opening the door to what yet may be, this rite provides one way for that to happen.

The rite provided here is not well suited to every divorcing couple, and, even with those for whom it is appropriate, it is important that it not be used prematurely. The rite is not a substitute for the hard work the couple must do to end their marriage well; rather, the rite is purposed in acknowledging that, in having performed that work well, the couple is now ready to separate peaceably and begin new, but separate, lives.

The rite is intended for use among close family and friends, some of whom may be reluctant to participate. Encourage participation by describing the couple's desire for the support of their friends and family in ending the relationship in a way that honors marriage and demonstrates their continuing respect for one another. A special effort should be made to include the couple's parents and children (even adult ones).

The rite is appropriately led by the community pastor or priest or a lay religious leader. Recruit a friend or family member to read the scripture lesson. So that they may prepare for their respective roles, make copies of the rite available in advance to the leader, the reader, and to both members of the couple.

The rite may appropriately be held in the community's worship space or at the private residence of someone other than the couple. Make copies of the rite available to all participants. The rite may be followed by a simple reception, but exercise care to avoid characterizing the gathering as a celebration.

Leader:	The Lord be with you!
All:	And also with you!
Leader:	God is our refuge and strength, a very present help in trouble.
All:	Therefore we will not fear,
Women:	Though the earth should change,
Men:	Though the mountains shake in the heart of the sea,
All:	Though its waters roar and foam, though the mountains tremble with its tumult.
Leader:	God is our refuge and strength,
All:	A very present help in trouble. *(Psalm 46:1–3)*
Leader:	*(addressing the community)* On _____ (date), family and friends of _____ and _____ had cause to celebrate their union in marriage. We are gathered together on this day to mark the dissolution of their marriage.
	Let us pray.
	God of our hopes, dreams, and promises, hear now the confessions of your children.
	A brief silence is observed for reflection.
	Holy and gracious God,
All:	We confess to you our failure to love one another as you have loved us, to forgive one another as you have forgiven us, and to become the people you intend for us to be. Heal our brokenness, assure us with your love, and comfort us with visions of the new creation you are fashioning for us and in us. We pray in the name of Jesus Christ, in whom we are assured of eternal refuge in you, Amen.
Reader:	A reading from St. Paul's letter to the Romans, the eighth chapter:

Who will separate us from the love of Christ? Will hardship, or distress, or persecution, or famine, or nakedness, or peril, or sword? No, in all these things we are more than conquerors through him who loved us. For I am convinced that neither death, nor life, nor angels, nor rulers, nor things present, nor things to come, nor powers, nor height, nor depth, nor anything else in all creation, will be able to separate us from the love of God in Christ Jesus our Lord. *(Romans 8:35, 37–39)*

The word of the Lord!

All: Thanks be to God!

Leader: In Christ, all experiences of sin and failure are ingredient to the new creation God is fashioning for us and in us.

All: In Christ, we are freed to begin again! Thanks be to God!

Leader: *(addressing the community)* Out of respect and concern for one another, _____ and _____ desire to dissolve their marriage in the presence of God and with the blessing of family and friends. Are you prepared to support them in the dissolution of their marriage?

Family
& Friends: *(addressing man and woman)* Your journey has been our journey. Even when we have not known how to be helpful, we have felt your sorrow and shared your pain. Although we do not fully understand your decision to dissolve your marriage, from this day forward, we pledge to love and support you in it.

Man
& Woman: *(addressing the community)* We have valued your companionship during this painful time, and we treasure your willingness to support us as we seek to build new, but separate, lives.

Leader: *(addressing the man and woman)* Before God and this community of your family and friends, we invite you to envision your relationship with each other from this day forward.

Time is allowed for the man and woman to express regrets regarding the demise of their marriage and to declare their commitment to a future relationship of honor and respect for one another.

Leader: *(addressing the community)* We have heard _____ and _____'s commitments. Will you pledge your love and support as they live out these commitments from this day forward?

Friends
& Family: We do, and we ask God to help and guide us.

If the man and woman share responsibilities and commitments to children, it would be appropriate for them at this time to affirm their covenant relationship with their children.

Leader: Go in peace to serve God and honor one another, from this day forward.

Woman: May God bless us and keep us.

Man: May God's face shine on us and be gracious to us.

All: May God look on us with favor and give us peace.

Leader: The peace of the Lord be with you always!

All: And also with you!

The rite concludes with a sharing of the peace.

Our Trust in You
Preparation for Surgery

Although surgeries are performed for a wide variety of routine and not-so-routine reasons and purposes, submitting oneself to surgery leaves almost everyone feeling vulnerable and anxious. This rite places those feelings about an approaching surgery within the context of God's abiding love and care.

The rite is intended for use within a small circle of close friends and family; when appropriate and feasible, it could also include members of the medical staff. The rite may be held either in the patient's home on the night prior to surgery or in the patient's hospital room just prior to surgery. Recruit a friend or family member to lead the rite and give him/her a copy of the rite in advance so that he/she may prepare for the role. Point out the need to select a prayer petition appropriate to the patient's situation or, if one is not provided in the rite, to prepare one that is.

When it is time to begin, invite participants to stand and form a circle around the person who will undergo surgery. Make copies of the rite available to all participants.

Leader: The Lord be with you!
All: And also with you!

Leader: O Lord, you have searched me and known me. You know when I lie down and when I rise up.
All: When I am afraid, I put my trust in you!

Leader: My flesh . . . may fail, but God is the strength of my heart and my portion forever.
All: If I trust in God, what can flesh do to me?

Leader: Where can I go from your spirit? Or where can I flee from your presence?
All: I am continually with you; you hold my right hand.

Leader:	If I take the wings of the morning and settle at the farthest limits of the sea,
All:	Even there your hand shall lead me and your right hand shall hold me fast.

Leader:	If I say, "Surely the darkness shall cover me, and the light around me become night,"
All:	Even the darkness is not dark to you; the night is as bright as the day, for darkness is as light to you.

Leader:	You hem me in, behind and before, and lay your hand upon me.
All:	When I am afraid, I put my trust in you! *(Psalm 56:3–4; 73:23, 26; 139:1–3, 5, 7, 9–12)*

Leader: *(addressing the community)* We are gathered in preparation for _____'s surgery, to acknowledge his/her fears, to remind him/her of God's presence, and to assure him/her of our support in prayer.

Let us pray.

Healing God, we praise you for the love with which you created _____ and by which you have sustained him/her throughout his/her life. As he/she faces surgery, give him/her a clear sense of your presence and strong assurance of your abiding love, that he/she may be at peace in you. God of mercy,

All: We put our trust in you!

Leader: Healing God, you have empowered those engaged in ministries of medicine with amazing knowledge and skill. As members of _____'s medical team prepare for his/her surgery, equip them with clear minds and steady hands, that their efforts may achieve the intended purpose. God of mercy,

All: We put our trust in you!

Leader: Healing God, you have fashioned our bodies as vessels to receive your love and grace.

Leader selects appropriate petitions from those provided or prepares a petition appropriate to the particular circumstance.

(when surgery is for the removal of an organ or limb)

> As _____ prepares for the removal of his/her _____, assure him/her that his/her body will continue to be the recipient of your blessing and a temple where your honor dwells.

(when surgery is for the removal of sexual organs)

> As _____ prepares for the removal of his/her _____, assure him/her that his/her sexuality will continue to be an expression of your goodness.

(when surgery is for the receipt of transplanted organs, tissues, or cells)

> As _____ prepares for surgery, enable him/her to receive with gratitude others' life-giving donation(s) of _____.

(when surgery is to correct or repair malfunction)

> As _____ prepares for surgery, fill him/her with hope for restoration of his/her _____.

(when surgery is to enhance fertility)

> As _____ prepares for surgery, give him/her confidence in your desire to satisfy the desires of all your children.

(when surgery is to curtail fertility)

> As _____ prepares for surgery, assure him/her with visions of your creative power at work within him/her.

(when surgery is for cancer)

> As _____ prepares for surgery, empower him/her with the assurance that nothing in life or death can separate us from your love.
>
> Hold him/her, we pray, in the security of your embrace, journey with him/her through this time of uncertainty, and guide him/her toward wholeness of life in you. God of mercy,

All: We put our trust in you!

Leader: Healing God, we are grateful for your gift of family and friends. Comfort those who wait and watch after _____'s well-being, that the assurance of your care may sustain them in patience and trust. God of mercy,

All: We put our trust in you!

Leader: In the name of your Son, the Great Physician of life, who taught us to pray:

(Traditional version)

> Our Father, who art in heaven,
> hallowed be thy name, thy kingdom come,
> thy will be done, on earth as it is in heaven.
> Give us this day our daily bread;
> and forgive us our trespasses
> as we forgive those who trespass against us.
> and lead us not into temptation,
> but deliver us from evil.

For thine is the kingdom, and the power,
and the glory, forever and ever. Amen.

or

(Contemporary version)

Our Father in heaven,
hallowed be your name,
your kingdom come,
your will be done,
on earth as in heaven
Give us today our daily bread.
Forgive our sins
as we forgive those
who sin against us.
Save us from the time of trial
and deliver us from evil.
For the kingdom, the power,
and the glory are yours,
now and forever. Amen.

Those present may place their hands on the patient's arms or shoulders.

Leader: May God bless you and keep you!
May God's face shine on you and be gracious to you!
May God look on you with favor and give you peace!

*The rite concludes with opportunity for personal expressions of
goodwill to the person undergoing surgery.*

I Will Be with You Always
Marking the Transition to an Assisted-Care Residence

As persons age, a diminishing capacity for self-care can make residence in an assisted-care facility a necessity, but rarely is that transition a cause for celebration. For those who have already experienced numerous significant losses (of loved ones, of mobility, of independence, and so forth), a move into assisted care can evoke powerful feelings of fear, grief, or anger. This rite is purposed in offering assurance of God's love and abiding presence in the midst of what may be a difficult transition.

The rite is intended for use in the room that the individual will occupy. Plans to use the rite should be coordinated in advance with the staff, who may be invited to have a representative participate. Although the size of the individual's personal space will limit the number of participants, the gathering should ideally include a representative circle of the individual's family and friends and, if possible, a representative of the individual's faith community. If the individual will be sharing a room with another resident, consider inviting that person's participation.

Although the rite may certainly be led by a friend or family member, it would also be appropriate to invite a representative of the faith community's homebound visitation ministry to lead the rite. Recruit friends or family members to read the brief passages from scripture and someone to find and present an appropriate memento. In order that the leader, reader(s), and presenter may have opportunity to prepare for their respective roles, provide them with a copy of the rite in advance. On the day of the rite, make copies available to all participants.

Leader: The Lord be with you!
All: And also with you!

Leader: O Lord, you have searched me and known me.
All: You know when I sit down and when I rise up; you discern my thoughts from far away.

| Leader: | You search out my path and my lying down, you are acquainted with all my ways. |
| All: | You hem me in, behind and before, and lay your hand upon me. |

| Leader: | Where can I go . . . [to] flee from your presence? If I ascend to heaven, |
| All: | You are there! |

| Leader: | If I take the wings of the morning . . . [to]the farthest limits of the sea, |
| All: | Even there your hand shall lead me, and your right hand shall hold me fast. |

Leader:	O Lord, you have searched me and known me.
All:	Your right hand shall hold me fast.
	(Psalm 139:1–3, 5, 7, 9–10)

Leader: *(addressing the community)* We are gathered in this place to share with _____ in a time of transition from his/her home/apartment/dwelling-with-family to life in this assisted-care residence. The significance of this transition is heightened by other life changes beyond his/her control, such as (name such factors as diminished physical strength or capacity for self-care, death of a spouse, inability of loved ones to attend to his/her care needs, and so forth). If we are honest, we must acknowledge that this transition marks a time of loss for him/her.

(addressing the person in transition) _____, what losses do you feel most strongly at this time?

Time is allowed for the individual making the transition to name some of the losses he/she will grieve. Depending on the mental capacity and personality of the individual, he/she may need to be gently prompted with simple, reflective statements like "_____, I wonder if you will miss your yard and flowers" or "I imagine you will miss having your cat Boots living with you." Care should be exercised so the individual will not feel obligated to disclose, pressured to share at someone else's pace, or overwhelmed by the cumulative magnitude of his/her losses. When this time of sharing has concluded, the rite continues.

Leader: Although transitions necessarily prompt moments of grief, they also contain elements of newness.

(addressing the person in transition) _____, how might this time of transition be experienced as a time of new beginnings?

Time is allowed for the individual and other participants to name some of the hopeful signs of his/her new living arrangement, stated in terms of their benefit to the person in transition. This might include opportunities to make new friends and explore new interests, living in pleasant surroundings where meals will be prepared for him/her, having his/her health concerns carefully monitored, and so forth. When the time of sharing has concluded, the rite continues.

Leader: *(addressing the person in transition)* We know, _____, that this room feels unfamiliar to you, so we want to ask God to bless this space and help you feel at home here.

The leader moves to the space where the individual's clothing and other belongings are kept and places his/her hand on it.

Reader: A reading from the gospel according to Matthew:

"Therefore I tell you," Jesus said, "do not worry about your life, what you will eat or what you will drink, or . . . what you will wear. Is not life more than food, and the body more than clothing? Look at the birds of the air; they neither sow nor reap nor gather into barns, and yet your heavenly Father feeds them. Consider the lilies of the field, how they grow; they neither toil nor spin, yet I tell you, even Solomon in all his glory was not clothed like one of these. Indeed your heavenly Father knows that you need all these things, . . . so do not worry about tomorrow." *(Matthew 6:25–26a, 28b–29, 32b–34a)*

The gospel of the Lord!

All: Thanks be to God!

All: May God bless this dresser/closet/cabinet, that it may remind _____ of God's constant care for all his/her needs.

The leader moves to the bedside lamp and places his/her hand on it.

Reader: Your word is a lamp to my feet and a light to my path. The unfolding of your words gives light [and] imparts understanding. Make your face shine upon your servant, and teach me your statutes.
(Psalm 119:105, 130, 135)

All: May God bless this lamp that _____ may be reminded of the brightness of God's presence.

The leader moves to the bedside chair and places his/her hand on it.

Reader: Thus says the Lord of hosts: Old men and old women shall again sit in the streets of Jerusalem, each with staff in hand because of their great age. They shall be my people and I will be their God, in faithfulness and in righteousness. *(Zechariah 8:4, 8b)*

All: May God bless this chair, that it may remind _____ that he/she sits in the midst of God's faithfulness.

The leader moves to the bed and places his/her hand on it.

Reader: Be gracious to me, [O Lord,] and hear my prayer. Let the light of your face shine on [me and] put gladness in my heart. I will both lie down and sleep in peace;

for you alone, O Lord, make me lie down in safety.
(*Psalm 4:1b, 6b–8*)

All: May God bless this bed, that it may remind _____ that every day is begun and ended in the shelter of your embrace.

Leader: With what shall we mark the blessing of God in this place?

Time is allowed for a friend or family member to present a gift to remind the individual of God's abiding presence (a cross, plaque, Bible, and so forth).

Leader: Let us pray.

God of every time and season, make your presence known to _____ as he/she begins his/her life in this space. Comfort him/her during this time of transition and encourage him/her with the assurance of your unchanging love, for you have promised:

All: I will be with you always.

Leader: God of endless possibility, open _____'s heart to the opportunities you will provide in this place for new relationships and experiences. Give him/her joy in the companionship of others and gratitude for the care he/she receives, trusting always in your promise:

All: I will be with you always.

Leader: God of all love and goodness, bless _____'s caregivers with compassion, that they may treat each person with dignity and respect. May their patience and understanding be signs of your love and concern for all people, who dwell securely in your promise:

All: I will be with you always.

Leader:	God of community, be with _____'s family and friends, that we may be mindful of the love that binds us as one in you. In our words and deeds of love, reveal the sureness of your promise:
All:	I will be with you always.
Leader:	God of all hopefulness, be with _____ in moments of discouragement in the midst of present and future life changes. Grounded in your faithfulness to your promises, give him/her courage for the present and confidence for a future life with you. In the name of Jesus, your Son, in whom your promises are fulfilled.
All:	Amen! Thanks be to God!
Leader:	*(addressing the person in transition)* And now, _____, receive the blessing of Almighty God:
All:	May God bless you and keep you! May God's face shine on you and be gracious to you! May God look on you with favor and give you peace!
Leader:	The peace of the Lord be with you always!
All:	And also with you!

The rite concludes with a sharing of the peace.

IV

COMFORT

Too Soon Ended
Marking Loss of a Pregnancy or the Death of an Infant

Although attention during the loss of a pregnancy or the death of an infant tends to focus on the mother, both mother and father are likely to experience feelings of deep grief and sorrow. Siblings, grandparents, and other family members and friends may also feel the loss deeply. Those touched by the loss may be aided in their grieving by this rite, which helps bring a sense of closure to the life too soon ended.

While some parents may have an immediate readiness for such closure, studies suggest that most will require a period of two to six weeks to arrive at a point of acceptance and release. This ritual may be used either at the time of loss (perhaps in the hospital room, with an intimate circle of family members) or at a later time (perhaps in the home nursery the parents were readying for their child, with a circle of close friends and family).

Go over the rite in advance with the parents and determine whether they would like an opportunity to name the child and whether they would like the time of remembrance to be one of oral sharing or silent reflection. Recruit to lead the rite someone other than a family member, perhaps a respected friend or religious leader who possesses the sensitivity to facilitate what may be an experience of emotional release. Recruit a friend or family member to read the scripture lesson. So that they may have opportunity to prepare for their respective roles, make copies of the rite available in advance to the leader, reader, and parents.

To prepare for the rite, arrange a few mementos (perhaps a sonogram or photograph, a blanket or article of clothing, or some other item acquired in anticipation of the young life) on a low table, perhaps with a lighted candle, cross, and open Bible. When it is time to begin, make copies of the rite available to all participants.

Leader: The Lord be with you!
All: And also with you!

Leader: O Lord, you have searched me and known me . . . you
           discern my thoughts from far away.

All:	You are acquainted with all my ways. Even before a word is on my tongue, O Lord, you know it completely.
Leader:	Where can I go from your spirit? Or where can I flee from your presence?
All:	If I ascend to heaven, you are there. If I make my bed in hell, you are there.
Leader:	If I take the wings of the morning and settle at the farthest limits of the sea, even there your hand shall lead me, and your right hand shall hold me fast.
All:	If I say, "Surely the darkness shall cover me, and the light around me become night," even the darkness . . . is as light to you.
Leader:	For it was you who formed my inward parts; you knit me together in my mother's womb.
All:	Your eyes beheld my unformed substance. In your book were written all the days that were formed for me. *(Psalm 139:1–4, 7–13, 16)*
Leader:	Hear also the word of the Lord spoken through the prophet Isaiah:

Leader: For I am about to create new heavens and a new earth; the former things shall not be remembered or come to mind. But be glad and rejoice forever in what I am creating; for I am about to create Jerusalem as a joy, and its people as a delight. I will rejoice in Jerusalem, and delight in my people; no more shall the sound of weeping be heard in it, or the cry of distress. No more shall there be in it an infant that lives but a few days, or an old person who does not live out a lifetime. *(Isaiah 65:17–20a)*

The word of the Lord!

All: Thanks be to God!

Leader:	(addressing the community) When God's creation of the new heavens and a new earth is complete, we will no longer need to gather to mourn the loss of a life too soon ended. But we come together on this day to acknowledge our sorrow over the loss of this life— precious to the mother who carried it, dear to the father who generated it, eagerly anticipated by all who hoped for it and dreamed of it. Every season will bring memories of this life too soon ended.
	(addressing the parents) By what name will we remember his/her presence in our lives?
Parent(s):	He/she will be known to us as _____.

If desired, the parent(s) may briefly explain the significance of the chosen name.

| Leader: | We remember before you, O God, the hopes and dreams we had for _____. |

A time of remembrance is observed, either a time of oral sharing or of silent reflection.

Leader:	Let us pray.
	You know, O God, the sorrows of our hearts and are present with us in our grief. Give us courage to commend _____ to your tender care. Use our grief to engender in us the certain hope that, in the power of your creative love, all things are ingredient to the new creation you are fashioning for us and in us. We pray in the name of Jesus, the beloved child you offered up in order that all might be claimed for newness of life in you,
All:	Amen! May it be so!

| Leader: | The peace of the Lord be with you always! |
| All: | And also with you! |

The rite concludes with a sharing of the peace.

Crushed in Spirit
Times of Disappointment

Even as we are called to share one another's joys, so are we also called to share one another's sorrows. This rite creates a place for acknowledgment of life's disappointments.

The rite is intended for use within an intimate circle of close family and friends. It would be appropriately used in conjunction with a Bible study, prayer group, or small group ministry meeting, or at a gathering called for this specific purpose.

Recruit one friend or family member to lead the rite and another to read the scripture lesson. Go over the rite with the person who has experienced a disappointment, alerting him/her to the place in the rite where he/she will have an opportunity to share the nature of the disappointment and its significance. So that they may be prepared for their respective roles, make copies of the rite available in advance to the leader, reader, and person who has experienced a disappointment.

When it is time to begin, invite participants to assemble in a close circle. Make copies of the rite available to all participants.

Leader: The Lord be with you!
All: And also with you!

Leader: Which of you desires life, and covets many days to enjoy good?
All: Many are the afflictions of the righteous, but the Lord rescues them from them all!

Leader: The eyes of the Lord are on the righteous, and his ears are open to their cry.
All: The Lord is near to the brokenhearted, and saves the crushed in spirit!

Leader: Weeping may linger for the night, but joy comes with the morning.
All: The Lord is near to the brokenhearted, and saves the crushed in spirit! *(Psalm 34:12, 15, 18–19; 30:5b)*

Reader: A reading from St. Paul's letter to the Galatians, the fifth and sixth chapters:

The fruit of the Spirit is love, joy, peace, patience, kindness, generosity, faithfulness, gentleness, and self-control. If we live by the Spirit, let us also be guided by the Spirit. Let us not become conceited, competing against one another, envying one another. Bear one another's burdens, and in this way you will fulfill the law of Christ. So then, whenever we have an opportunity, let us work for the good of all, and especially for those of the family of faith.
(Galatians 5:22, 25; 6:2, 10)

The word of the Lord!

All: Thanks be to God!

Leader: Even as we are called to share one another's joys, so also are we called to share one another's sorrows. We are gathered to embrace one who is crushed in spirit.

(addressing the one who has experienced disappointment) _____, what burden will you allow this community to share?

Time is allowed for a brief sharing of the disappointment and its significance for the individual. When the sharing is concluded, the rite continues.

Leader: *(addressing the community)* How will we receive _____'s disappointment?

All: We stand with you in the darkness of your crushed spirit and will journey with you back into the light!

Leader: Let us pray.

God of the brokenhearted, make your presence known to _____ in his/her experience of shattered hopes and broken dreams. Comfort him/her with assurances of your love and, in time, awaken him/her to the light of the new day you are fashioning for him/her. In this time of disappointment,

All: Uphold, we pray, the crushed in spirit!

Leader: God of the brokenhearted, make your presence known to each of us as we experience the many heartaches of life. Make your comfort known to us in our sharing of one another's burdens and in our labors for the good of all. In times of disappointment,

All: Sustain, we pray, the crushed in spirit!

Leader: God of the brokenhearted, make your presence known to those who bear their burdens in isolation. Give them courage to voice their sorrows and give us compassion to hear them. In the time of disappointment,

All: Set free, we pray, the crushed in spirit!

Leader: God of the brokenhearted, who offered up your Son to shoulder our every burden, we cast our cares on you, knowing that you care for us.

All: Amen! May it be so!

The community may form a circle around the one who has experienced disappointment and place their hands on his/her shoulders.

Leader: *(addressing the one who has experienced disappointment)*

May God bless you and keep you in this time of broken heart and crushed spirit!

May God's face shine on you and be gracious to you as you seek courage for future days!

May God look on you with favor and give you peace in the hope for a brighter tomorrow!

Hands are withdrawn.

Leader: The peace of the Lord be with you!
All: And also with you!

The rite concludes with a sharing of the peace.

In Wisdom You Made Them
Marking the Death of a Pet

Even as pets bless our lives with companionship and joy, their deaths evoke in us feelings of grief and loss. This rite offers those who have experienced the death of a pet an opportunity to give voice to those feelings of grief and loss and to be reminded of God's love for all creation.

The rite is intended for use among a small, intimate circle of family and friends who knew the pet and who appreciate the valued place the pet occupied in the life of its owner(s). The rite may be held in a location where the pet's presence was experienced and will be particularly missed (for example, in the back yard, in a favorite park or open space, gathered around the pet's home, in the place where the pet's remains have been laid to rest). If desired, have a box or basket available to collect mementos of the pet.

Recruit a friend or family member to lead the rite, someone who is close enough to empathize with the feelings of loss but not so close that their own grief would impair their leadership. Alert participants in advance that they will have an opportunity during the rite to share memories and/or a memento of the pet's life.

So that he/she may prepare for his/her role, make a copy of the rite available in advance to the leader.

When it is time to begin, invite participants to assemble at the selected location. Make copies of the rite available to all participants.

Leader:	The Lord be with you!
All:	And also with you!
Leader:	O Lord, how manifold are your works; in wisdom you have made them all.
All:	The earth is full of your creatures; they look to you to give them their food in due season.
Leader	When you open your hand, they are filled with good things; when you send forth your spirit, they are created.
All:	When you take away their breath, they die and return to their dust. *(Psalm 104:24, 27, 29, 30)*

Leader:	To God, who in every time and season cares for the earth and all its creatures,
All:	Be glory and honor, now and forever!
Leader:	*(addressing the community)* One of the ways we are sustained in God's great love is through special relationships with pets. On this occasion, we gather to celebrate the life of _____. What memories will we share on this day?

Time is allowed for participants to share memories of the deceased pet's life. When the sharing has concluded the rite continues.

Leader:	With what memento(s) will we continue to hold _____ in our hearts?

Time is allowed for a sharing of mementos, such as photographs, tags or collars, and so forth. When the mementos have been shared, the rite continues.

Leader:	Let us pray.
	We give thanks, O God, for the gift of _____'s life and his/her presence in our lives. Console us in our loss and, in time, make our memories of _____ a source of comfort. Give us courage to entrust _____ to your tender care, knowing that, in every time and season, you use the cycles of life and death, joy and sorrow, beginnings and endings to renew your creation and restore all creation to you.
All:	In the name of Christ, we pray, Amen.
Leader:	The peace of the Lord be with you always!
All:	And also with you!

The rite concludes with a sharing of the peace.

The Shadow of Your Wings
Marking a Time of Natural Disaster

Because our culture cultivates the presumption that humankind has the ability to control the forces of nature, our experiences of natural disaster are often complicated by intense feelings of inadequacy and failure. This rite invites movement from preoccupation with self to heightened awareness of God's presence in, and authority over, even the most chaotic forces of nature.

The rite is intended for impromptu use among those who find themselves together during a time of natural disaster and is, therefore, purposefully designed to be inclusive of a variety of faith expressions. Recruit someone with a calming presence to lead the rite, a second person to read the brief scripture lesson. Encourage them to take a moment to look over the rite and to center themselves in preparation for their leadership roles.

When it is time to begin, invite participants to stand and gather in close proximity to one another. If possible, make copies of the rite available to all participants. When that is not feasible, recruit someone to partner with the leader in reading the "all" responses. Encourage participants to echo (that is, repeat line by line) the responses to the prayer petitions (marked by ::).

Leader:	The Lord be with you!
All:	And also with you!
Leader:	Be merciful to me, O God, be merciful to me, for in you my soul takes refuge.
All:	In the shadow of your wings, I will take refuge, until the destroying storms pass me by.
Leader:	Though the earth should change,
All:	Though the mountains shake in the heart of the sea,
Leader:	Though its waters roar and foam, though the mountains tremble with its tumult,
All:	Your steadfast love, O Lord, extends to the heavens, your faithfulness to the clouds.

Leader:	My soul takes refuge in you, O God.
All:	Hide me in the shadow of your wings!
	(Psalm 36:5; 46:2–3; 57:1)

Leader: *(addressing the community)* At this time of natural disaster, we are faced with painful reminders that the forces of nature are beyond our control. We gather together to seek refuge in God's abiding love for us, to be assured of God's authority in the midst of nature's chaos, and to pray for strength and courage in the face of pain and sorrow.

Reader: A reading from Isaiah, the fortieth and forty-first chapters:

Have you not known? Have you not heard? The Lord is the everlasting God, the Creator of the ends of the earth. He does not ... grow weary, his understanding is unsearchable. He gives power to the faint and strengthens the powerless. Those who wait for the Lord shall renew their strength, they shall mount up with wings like eagles, they shall run and not be weary, they shall walk and not faint. Do not fear, for I am with you, do not be afraid, for I am your God. I will strengthen you, I will help you, I will uphold you with my victorious right hand.
(Isaiah 40:28b–29, 31; 41:10)

The word of the Lord!

All: Thanks be to God.

Leader: Let us pray.

Mindful, O God, of your dominion over all creation, we long for the assurance of your abiding love.

A brief silence is observed for silent reflection.

For those whose lives are in harm's way, we pray:

All:	::Protect them under the shadow of your wings!
Leader:	For those who have been injured or whose loved ones have been killed, we pray:
All:	::Comfort them under the shadow of your wings!
Leader:	For those whose losses leave them without safety, refuge, food, or clothing, we pray:
All:	::Shelter them under the shadow of your wings!
Leader:	For those who will bring aid and seek to restore order in the midst of chaos, we pray:
All:	::Guard them under the shadow of your wings!
Leader:	For those who seek courage to face an uncertain future, we pray:
All:	::Renew their strength under the shadow of your wings!
Leader:	For those who will journey together on the long road toward renewal, we pray:
All:	::Bind us as one under the shadow of your wings!
Leader:	For those whose specific concerns we name before you now . . .

Time is allowed for participants to briefly state particular prayer concerns.

Leader:	For these and for whatever else you see that we have need of, we pray,
All:	In the name of Jesus Christ, our refuge and strength, Amen.
Leader:	May God bless us and keep us,
All:	That the shadow of God's wings may comfort and sustain us!
Leader:	May God's face shine on us and be gracious to us,

All:	That the shadow of God's wings may give us strength and courage!
Leader: All:	May God look on us with favor and give us peace, that the shadow of God's wings may enfold us in love!
Leader: All:	The peace of the Lord be with you always! And also with you!

The rite concludes with a sharing of the peace.

Our Refuge and Strength
When a Loved One Is Seriously Ill

The serious illness of a loved one leaves us feeling helpless and ineffective. This rite acknowledges, within the context of God's love for us, that God alone is able to effect healing and bring wholeness of body, mind, and spirit.

The rite is intended for use among a small circle of close family and friends, but, when appropriate and feasible, it may also include medical staff or home health-care workers. It may be held in the loved one's residence or in some other place where the loved one is receiving care. Recruit one friend or family member to lead the rite and another to read the scripture lesson. Encourage them to take a few moments to familiarize themselves with their respective roles.

When it is time to begin, invite those present to stand and form a circle around their loved one. Make copies of the rite available to all participants.

Leader:	The Lord be with you!
All:	And also with you!
Leader:	I lift up my eyes to the hills—from where will my help come?
All:	God is our refuge and strength, a very present help in trouble!
Leader:	He will not let your foot be moved; he who keeps you will . . . neither slumber nor sleep.
All:	God is our refuge and strength, a very present help in trouble!
Leader:	The sun shall not strike you by day, nor the moon by night.
All:	God is our refuge and strength, a very present help in trouble!
Leader:	The Lord will keep your going out and your coming in from this time on and forevermore.

All:	God is our refuge and strength, a very present help in trouble! *(Psalm 46:1; 121:1, 3, 6, 8)*
Reader:	A reading from the gospel according to Matthew, the eighth chapter:

When Jesus entered Peter's house, he saw his mother-in-law lying in bed with a fever; he touched her hand, and the fever left her, and she got up and began to serve him. That evening they brought to him many who were possessed with demons; and he cast out the spirits with a word, and cured all who were sick. This was to fulfill what had been spoken through the prophet Isaiah, "He took our infirmities and bore our diseases." *(Matthew 8:14–17)*

The gospel of the Lord!

All:	Thanks be to God!
Leader:	*(addressing the community)* Because we trust that God is, indeed, our refuge and strength, we have come together in this place to seek healing for _____. We come with a recognition that God's healing is experienced in a variety of ways—as restoration to health, as relief from pain, as liberation from suffering, and as peace in the face of death.

Those present may lay their hands on the person who seeks healing.

Leader:	Let us pray.

O God, refuge of the sick and strength of the weary, embrace _____ in your tender care. Strengthen him/her with a clear sense of your presence. Equip his/her medical team with compassion and insight. Give courage to those of us who long for his/her restoration and healing. We pray in the name of Christ our Lord, who alone has the power to heal our bodies, soothe our minds, and calm our spirits, Amen.

Hands are withdrawn.

| Leader: | *(addressing the one who seeks healing)* May the God who is our refuge and strength, |
| All: | Bless you and keep you! |

| Leader: | May the God who is our refuge and strength, |
| All: | Make his face to shine on you and be gracious to you! |

| Leader: | May the God who is our refuge and strength, |
| All: | Look on you with favor and give you peace! |

*The rite concludes with opportunity for participants to speak
a word of peace and blessing to the one who seeks healing.*

Deliver Us, O Lord
When Violence Has Been Experienced

Experiences of violence shatter the familiar, trusted patterns of our lives. Confidence in personal security is exposed as the illusion it has always been. A victim's view of the world is changed in ways that family and friends cannot begin to comprehend. Uncertain of how to be supportive or helpful, loved ones may find it easier to avoid the victim or pretend that nothing has changed. Victims may experience their loved ones' avoidance as desertion, their pretense as a trivialization of the violence they experienced. All these responses can be exacerbated by the nagging fear that God may not be the reliable presence they have trusted God to be.

This rite invites recognition that violence is a universal human experience. Bringing the victim together with his/her friends and family members in a place where God can speak to the shattering effects of violence in his/her life and relationships, it provides a safe place for the victim to share what he/she chooses to reveal of his/her experience and the effect that the experience is having in his/her life. It also offers a place where friends and family members may embrace their loved one's pain, convey their concern, and commit to accompanying their loved one on his/her road toward recovery. In considering this rite, be aware that, while violence conjures up images of physical brutality, it has other equally harmful manifestations; sexual abuse, verbal abuse, prejudice, and discrimination are all examples of violence that inflicts painful injury.

This rite is intended for use within an intimate circle of close family and friends, but be aware that our natural inclination to deny pain in self and others will produce in some persons a reluctance to participate (gently encourage their participation, but do not abuse them with the violence of coercion). Select a site that honors the victim's preference (which may be some place closely linked to his/her experience of violence or one far removed from it).

Recruit a friend, family member, or counselor to lead the rite. Recruit another friend or family member to read the scripture lesson. Go over the rite with the victim, pointing out the opportunity for sharing his/her experience. Discuss his/her comfort in being touched (or even being closely surrounded) during the blessing at the conclusion of the rite and take steps to ensure that his/her wishes are honored. So that they may prepare for their respective roles, make copies of the rite available in advance to the leader, reader, and victim.

When it is time to begin, invite participants to stand and gather as one community with the victim. Make copies of the rite available to all participants.

Leader:	The Lord be with you!
All:	And also with you!

Leader:	Deliver me, O Lord, from evildoers.
All:	Protect me from those who are violent; guard me from the hands of the wicked.

Leader:	O Lord, heal me, for [I am] shaking with terror; I am weary with my moaning.
All:	How long must I bear pain in my soul, and have sorrow in my heart all day long?

Leader:	Depart from me, all you workers of evil, for the Lord has heard the sound of my weeping.
All:	The Lord has heard my supplication; the Lord accepts my prayer. *(Psalm 6:2, 8–9; 13:2; 140:1)*

Reader:	A reading from the gospel according to Mark, the fifteenth chapter:
	"What then," Pilate asked the crowd, "do you wish me to do with the man you call the King of the Jews?" They shouted back, "Crucify him!" Pilate asked them, "Why, what evil has he done?" But they shouted all the more, "Crucify him!" So Pilate, wishing to satisfy the crowd . . . handed Jesus over to be crucified.
	It was nine o'clock in the morning when they crucified him . . . When it was noon, darkness came over the whole land until three in the afternoon. At three o'clock, Jesus cried out with a loud voice, saying, "My God, my God, why have you forsaken me?" Then

Jesus gave a loud cry and breathed his last.
(*Mark 15:12–15, 25, 33–34, 37*)

The gospel of the Lord!

Leader: (*addressing the community*) When violence against body, mind, or spirit invades our lives, the enduring effects of our violation threaten to rob us of our sense of personal security, our ability to trust, our confidence in self, our joy in the present and hope for the future, our faith in the reliability of God's care and protection. Through our presence and prayers, we extend support to our brother/sister, whose life has been touched by violence.

(*addressing the one who has been violated*)
_____ , what will you share with us of your experience?

Time is allowed for a brief description of the violence and a sharing of how the experience has violated his/her physical, emotional, or spiritual well-being. When the time of sharing has concluded, the rite continues.

Leader: (*addressing the community*) How will we receive _____ and his/her experience?
All: We embrace your pain! We share your tears! We promise to accompany you on your journey toward healing!

Leader: Let us pray.

Source of all mercy and God of all consolation, make your presence known to _____ . Calm his/her fears, heal his/her pain, assure him/her of your love, and protect him/her from further violation, that he/she may recover from the lingering effects of his/her experience and regain her confidence in your care. From evil's hold on him/her,

All: Deliver him/her, Lord!

Leader: We are in anguish over _____'s ex-
                perience of violence and long to be instruments of
                healing in his/her life. Give us courage to be present
                with him/her in his/her pain, wisdom to know when
                to speak and when to listen, and readiness to provide
                help as it is requested. From our inclinations to avoid
                pain in self and others,
All: Deliver us, O Lord!

Leader: We long for your protection from the violence of this
                world, and our faith is shaken when that protection
                seems unavailable to us. Use your Son's experience of
                violence to remind us that, although you do not
                guarantee your children an escape from violence, you
                do promise to be present in our pain and to accom-
                pany us in our journey through violent experiences.
                From doubts about the faithfulness of your compan-
                ionship,
All: Deliver us, O Lord!

Leader: Although you have promised that all things will work
                together for good for those who love you, we glimpse
                no sign of goodness in _____'s ex-
                perience of violence. Even as you bring healing to
                his/her body, mind, and spirit, so also open his/her
                heart to future revelations of goodness in his/her life.
                From the belief that experiences of violence speak the
                decisive word in our lives,
All: Deliver us, O Lord!

Leader: How well we know that violence begets violence and
                that the perpetrators of violence have often them-
                selves been the victims of it. Break the cycle by giving
                us the courage and strength to take stands against all
                acts of physical, emotional, and spiritual violence, no
                matter how trivial they may seem. From words,
                deeds, and attitudes that fail to honor the holiness of
                all life,

All: Deliver us, O Lord!

Leader: We know that, throughout this world, there are many brothers and sisters for whom violence is a regular occurrence. Use _____'s experience of violence to remind us of our kinship with all victims of violence and to inspire us to stand in solidarity with them against the individuals and systems that perpetrate violence. From presumptions that violence is more acceptable in the lives of others than it is in our own,

All: Deliver us, O Lord!

Leader: We pray in the name of your Son, Jesus the Christ, whose victory over the violence of human sin assures us of eternal life in harmony with you, Amen.

Those gathered may encircle the one recovering from an experience of violence. If that person is open to human contact, participants may place their hands on his/her head or shoulders.

Leader: May God bless you and keep you.
                     May God's face shine on you and be gracious to you.
                     May God look on you with favor and give you peace.

Hands are withdrawn.

Leader: The peace of the Lord be with you always!
All: And also with you!

The rite concludes with a sharing of the peace.

Yet Shall We Live
When a Loved One Is Nearing Death

Anticipatory grief for a loved one nearing death can so distract us that we are unable to lay claim to the comforts of our faith. This rite reconnects participants with God's promise that death will not be the final word on our existence.

The rite is intended for use within an intimate circle of close family and friends but, when it is appropriate and feasible, medical staff may also be invited to participate. The rite may be held in the loved one's home or in whatever place he/she is receiving care. Recruit one friend or family member to lead the rite and another to read the scripture lesson. Encourage the leader and reader to take a moment to look over the rite and prepare for their respective roles.

When it is time to begin, encourage those gathered to stand and form a circle around their loved one. Make copies of the rite available to all participants.

Leader:	The Lord be with you!
All:	And also with you!
Leader:	O that my words were written down; O that they were inscribed in a book!
All:	For I know that my Redeemer lives, that at the last day he will stand upon the earth!
Leader:	[I know that]after my skin has been thus destroyed, then in my flesh I shall see God!
All:	I shall see [God] on my side and my eyes shall behold [him], and not another! *(Job 19:23, 25–27)*
Reader:	A reading from the gospel according to John, the eleventh chapter:
	Now a certain man was ill, Lazarus of Bethany, the village of Mary and her sister Martha. So the sisters sent a message to Jesus, "Lord, he whom you love is ill."

When Jesus arrived, he found that Lazarus had already been in the tomb four days. When Martha heard that Jesus was coming, she went and met him, while Mary stayed at home. Martha said to Jesus, "Lord, if you had been here, my brother would not have died. But even now I know that God will give you whatever you ask of him."

Jesus said to her, "Your brother will rise again." Martha said to him, "I know that he will rise again in the resurrection on the last day." Jesus said to her, "I am the resurrection and the life. Those who believe in me, even though they die, will live, and everyone who lives and believes in me will never die."
(John 11:1, 3, 17, 20–26)

The gospel of the Lord!

All: Thanks be to God!

Those gathered may join hands in a circle around their loved one.

Leader: Let us pray.

     Gracious God, who created _____,
     enfold him/her in tender care and fashion him/her for eternal life. God, in your mercy,
All: Hear our prayer!

Leader: Gracious God, who redeemed _____,
     forgive his/her sins and journey with him/her into the joy of the salvation prepared for him/her. God, in your mercy,
All: Hear our prayer!

Leader: Gracious God, who sustained _____
     throughout his/her life, comfort him/her and give him/her peace. God, in your mercy,
All: Hear our prayer!

Leader:	Those who believe in me, even though they die, will live. *(John 11:25)*
All:	Thanks be to God!
Leader:	Jesus, remember us in your kingdom and teach us to pray:
All:	*(traditional version)*

Our Father, who art in heaven,
hallowed be thy name, thy kingdom come,
thy will be done, on earth as it is in heaven.
Give us this day our daily bread;
and forgive us our trespasses
as we forgive those who trespass against us.
and lead us not into temptation,
but deliver us from evil.
For thine is the kingdom, and the power,
and the glory, forever and ever. Amen.

or

(contemporary version)

Our Father in heaven,
hallowed be your name,
your kingdom come,
your will be done,
on earth as in heaven
Give us today our daily bread.
Forgive our sins
as we forgive those
who sin against us.
Save us from the time of trial
and deliver us from evil.
For the kingdom, the power,
and the glory are yours,
now and forever. Amen.

Those gathered may lay their hands on their loved one.

Leader: _____, child of God, may you rest in peace and dwell forever in paradise with God. In the name of the Triune God, Father, Son, and Holy Spirit, Amen.

Hands are withdrawn.

The rite concludes with a vigil of silent prayer or, if desired, with the reading of scripture and the singing of hymns.

A Place Prepared
When Life-Support Is Removed

Few decisions exact greater anguish or require greater courage than the decision to discontinue life support for someone we hold dear. Those entrusted with that decision are advised to seek out the trusted counsel of a pastor, priest, or chaplain.

When faced with the enactment of a decision to discontinue life support, this rite can offer encouragement and support for those affected by it. Drawing assurance from Jesus' promise of a dwelling place prepared for us, the rite appropriately couches the decision as a surrendering of the loved one to God. The rite is intended for use among an intimate circle of close family and friends but, when it is appropriate and feasible, medical staff may also be invited to participate. It is held in the place where the loved one is receiving care.

Be aware that it is rarely possible to schedule a specific time for removing life support, so it's best not to become preoccupied with coordinating the use of this rite with that specific action. It might also be helpful to advise those gathered that, even after support has been discontinued, their loved one may linger for a time.

The rite may be led by the pastor, priest, or chaplain who has provided support during the decision-making process or by a trusted lay religious leader. Invite a friend or family member to read the brief scripture lesson. So that they may prepare for their respective leadership roles, make copies of the rite available in advance to the leader and the reader. When it is time to begin, invite participants to stand and form a circle around the loved one. Make copies of the rite available to all participants.

Leader:	The Lord be with you!
All:	And also with you!
Reader:	A reading from the gospel according to John, the fourteenth chapter:

> And Jesus said, "Do not let your hearts be troubled. Believe in God, believe also in me. In my Father's house there are many dwelling places. If it were not

so, would I have told you that I go to prepare a place for you? And if I go and prepare a place for you, I will come again and will take you to myself, so that where I am, there you may be also." (*John 14:1–3*)

The gospel of the Lord!

All: Thanks be to God!

Those gathered may join hands in a circle around their loved one.

Leader: Let us pray.

Heavenly Father, whose love for us is greater than life and death, make your presence known to _____ as we prayerfully surrender him/her to your tender care. Guide him/her safely homeward and joyfully welcome him/her in that place you have lovingly prepared for all your children. God, in your mercy,

All: Hear our prayer.

Leader: Son of God, by whose death and resurrection we are claimed for eternal life with you, make your presence known to us in our decision to discontinue the supports that stand between _____ and eternal life with you. Give us peace with our decision, comfort in our grief, and hope in your promise of a joyful reunion in that place you have lovingly prepared for all your children. God, in your mercy,

All: Hear our prayer!

Leader: Spirit of God, comforter of those who mourn, make your presence known to those who are feeling keenly the loss of this loved one. Console us in our grief, sustain us in our sorrow, and assure us with your promise of eternal life with you in that place you have lovingly prepared for all your children. God, in your mercy,

All:	Hear our prayer!
Leader:	Triune God, how well we know that all hearts are restless until they are at rest in you. Into your hands, we now commend _____. In your own time, receive him/her into the arms of your mercy and blessed rest in you. In the name of Christ, we pray,
All:	Amen.
Leader:	Lord, remember us in your kingdom, and teach us to pray:
All:	*(traditional version)*

Our Father, who art in heaven,
hallowed be thy name, thy kingdom come,
thy will be done, on earth as it is in heaven.
Give us this day our daily bread;
and forgive us our trespasses
as we forgive those who trespass against us.
and lead us not into temptation,
but deliver us from evil.
For thine is the kingdom, and the power,
and the glory, forever and ever. Amen.

or

(contemporary version)

Our Father in heaven,
hallowed be your name,
your kingdom come,
your will be done,
on earth as in heaven
Give us today our daily bread.
Forgive our sins
as we forgive those
who sin against us.

Save us from the time of trial
and deliver us from evil.
For the kingdom, the power,
and the glory are yours,
now and forever. Amen.

Those gathered may lay their hands on their loved one.

Leader: May God bless you and keep you.
            May God's face shine on you and be gracious to you.
            May God look on you with favor and give you peace.

            In the name of the Father, and of the Son, and of the
            Holy Spirit, Amen.

Hands may be withdrawn.

*The rite concludes with a time of silent prayer or, if desired,
the reading of scripture and/or the singing of hymns.*

Neither Death nor Life
Marking the Anniversary of a Loved One's Death

In the lives of those who have lost a close friend or family member, the anniversary of the loved one's death is often an occasion for fresh experience of grief, and those feelings can be exacerbated by the perception that their loved one has been forgotten. This rite honors the significance of those feelings, while encouraging the bereaved to negotiate (or affirm) movement to a place where grief is understood as ingredient to life, with memory becoming a source of comfort and consolation.

All human relationships encompass elements of brokenness, but, when a death occurs, our inclination is to repress or deny those aspects of our experience of the deceased. This rite provides an opportunity to release lingering feelings of anger, bitterness, offense, or resentment, in order that grief for the loved one may achieve peaceful resolution.

This rite may appropriately be used at any gathering of close friends and family members, but it is especially powerful when combined with a visit to the deceased loved one's final resting place. In consideration of fresh feelings of grief and loss, make a point of alerting all participants in advance that they will have an opportunity to share memories of the loved one. Encourage a few participants to offer humorous or light-hearted memories, so that other participants may feel permission to offer a range of memories and recollections.

In order that all participants may have the opportunity to fully experience the rite, recruit a trusted person from outside the immediate circle of family and close friends to lead the rite. Recruit one or two friends or family members to read the scripture lessons. So that they may prepare for their roles, make copies of the rite available in advance to the leader and reader(s).

When it is time to begin, make copies of the rite available to all participants.

Leader: The Lord be with you!
All: And also with you!

| Leader: | Out of the depths I cry to you, O Lord, hear my voice! |
| All: | Let your ears be attentive, [O Lord,] to the voice of my supplications. |

| Leader: | I wait for the Lord; . . . in his word I hope. My soul waits for the Lord more than those who watch for the morning. |
| All: | Out of the depths I cry to you; O Lord, hear my voice! *(Psalm 130:1–2, 5–6)* |

Leader: *(addressing the community)* In the gospel according to John, we read that when Jesus arrived at the tomb of his friend Lazarus, he began to weep. The biblical text does not say why Jesus cried, but those of us gathered together on this day require no explanation. We have known the grief of losing a loved one to death and have shed tears that mourn the absence of one dear to us. Jesus, who himself knew such grief and loss, hears our cries and is attentive to our voice.

Reader #1: A reading from the holy gospel according to John, the fourteenth chapter:

Jesus said, "Do not let your hearts be troubled. Believe in God, believe also in me. In my Father's house there are many dwelling places. If it were not so, would I have told you that I go to prepare a place for you? And if I go and prepare a place for you, I will come again and will take you to myself, so that where I am, there you may be also." *(John 14:1–3)*

The gospel of the Lord!

All: Thanks be to God!

Leader: *(addressing the community)* We gather in this place, secure in Jesus' promise that he has gone to prepare a place for us, a place where we will reside forever in God's love and in communion with all the saints of God. And yet, even as we celebrate this promise of life secure in God, we also grieve our separation from this one who has gone before us. In one sense, our grief is unending, for we will always feel the void of _____'s absence. But, in another sense, life goes on, and even as the earth cycles through the seasons, our grief moves through stages that begin to make our losses bearable.

As we journey with our grief, there comes a time when our memories, once a source of such pain, become a source of consolation and comfort. What memories will we share, that those who grieve _____'s death may be comforted?

Time is allowed for a sharing of memories. When the sharing concludes, the rite continues.

Leader: Blessed be _____'s memory among us!

All: Thanks be to God!

Leader: *(addressing the community)* Because of sin, all relationships show signs of human brokenness. What lingering feelings of disappointment or regret, anger or bitterness, are ready to be surrendered to God and laid to rest on this day?

A brief silence is observed to allow for the release of lingering feelings to God's all-embracing love.

Leader: May we have courage in surrendering all to God's merciful care and claim peace for our memories of _____ .

Reader #2:   A reading from Paul's letter to the Romans, the eighth chapter:

Who will separate us from the love of Christ? Will hardship, or distress, or persecution, or famine, or nakedness, or peril, or sword? No, in all these things we are more than conquerors through him who loved us. For I am convinced that neither death, nor life, nor angels, nor rulers, nor things present, nor things to come, nor powers, nor height, nor depth, nor anything else in all creation, will be able to separate us from the love of God in Christ Jesus our Lord. *(Romans 8:35, 37–39)*

The word of the Lord!

All: Thanks be to God!

Leader: Let us pray.

God of all that was, is, and yet shall be, make your presence known among us, that we may discover peace beyond our tears and hope beyond our sorrows. In the name of Jesus, your Son our Lord, in whom we find enduring assurance that neither death nor life can separate us from your great love for us.

All: Amen! May it be so!

Leader: The peace of the Lord be with you always!
All: And also with you!

The rite concludes with a sharing of the peace.

About the Author

Author Linda W. Henke's interest in ritual has evolved gradually over a period of several years.

As an ordained minister in the Evangelical Lutheran Church in America, Henke has become increasingly aware that our culture's hunger for ritual far exceeds the availability of resources that speak to that hunger. *Marking Time* is the natural marriage of her background as a journalist (bachelor's and master's degrees in journalism and a successful public relations career) and her more recent experiences as a parish pastor, preacher, and seminar leader.

Henke previously authored *From the Seeds That Were Sown*, a self-published collection of devotional reflections on her experiences in preparation for ordained ministry, as well as numerous newspaper and magazine articles and book reviews. She has also served as a reviewer for lectionary-based curricula published by Living the Good News, Inc. She serves as pastor of Saint Peter Lutheran Church, Englewood, Colorado.